SHE WORKS HIS WAY
DEVOTIONALS
for the working woman

SHE WORKS HIS WAY

100 She Works HIS Way Devotionals for the Working Woman
Volume Two

©2019 Myers Cross Training
His Way Resources, Inc.
Cover Art, Design ©2019 Erica Zoller Creative, LLC

ISBN: 978-0-9964009-9-2

ACKNOWLEDGMENTS

To our families, thank you for daily reminding us that being your wife/mom is our greatest earthly gift. We appreciate your constant love and encouragement to be the women God created us to be.

James, Noah, Cole, + Shea Myers

Kent, Kennedi + Lizzie Phoebus

Jason, Harrison, Jonah, + Christian Patton

Colston, Hadley + Willow Copeland

John Hottle

Sam, Harper + Weezy Pineda

Andy, Emery + Hayden Zoller

To the she works His way community, thank you for the example that you are to us: in faith, in family, and in work. We love serving Jesus with you!

FOREWORD

. . . .

It's difficult to find business training you can fully trust. Not impossible.
But it's hard.

Why? Because if we don't share priorities, I will probably have to do some
serious filtering of your information before I can actually apply anything.

I want to learn from someone who defines success as obeying God, no
matter what.

I want to learn from someone who will remind me to prayerfully consider
my season of life – not just any available opportunity.

I want to learn from someone who uses their knowledge and experience
to positively impact the lives of others.

I want to learn from someone who reminds me to work for the "well
done, my good and faithful servant" – not the earthly recognition or
worldly rewards.

Can you relate? If you can, sweet friend, take a deep breath. That's
exactly our mission. We're not perfect, and we'll never claim to be. But
we know that His way is perfect, which is why our goal is never to point
you to us, but to lead you to Him.

We want to be that business training you can trust - no filter required.
Here's our commitment to you:

DEPENDENT *on god*   DEDICATED *to family*   EFFECTIVE *in our work*   COMMITTED *to the gospel*

DEPENDENT ON GOD
Gifts, talents, and abilities are real, but the One who put them in us is even
more real. Our goal is to be women who rely on God, not our gifting.

DEDICATED TO FAMILY
Our job may fluctuate throughout life, but we never have to question
the assignments God has given only to us. You are your husband's only
wife, and you are your children's only mother. Your family is your greatest

opportunity for Kingdom impact and significance. Daily, we remind one another of the high calling God has given each of us at home.

EFFECTIVE IN OUR WORK
Excellence matters to God, so excellence should matter to us. But it takes more than mere excellence or skill to be effective; it requires our willingness and ability to pass on our wisdom and experience to others. Our goal is never to wow you with our ability, but to help you duplicate the skills and systems that have worked for us in your work.

COMMITTED TO THE GOSPEL
In this post-modern world, it's become far too common for leaders to choose Jesus as part of their "brand." But Jesus isn't supposed to be part of our lives; we're supposed to live our whole lives surrendered to Him. Rather than using His name to push our own agenda, we're women committed to using our gifts and abilities to join in His agenda.

If you're a woman juggling the priorities of faith, family, and work, we see you. We get you. And most of all, we are FOR YOU!

Here's the truth: merely balancing your life will never work. You were divinely designed to put God first so He can order everything else (Matthew 6:33). *she works His way* exists to gather women just like you -- women who are committed to Christ, family and business...*in that order*.

It's our joy and honor to serve Kingdom-driven women through our annual conference, membership community, app, and business tools. Rather than simply teaching business strategies and sprinkling in Scripture to support it, the majority of She Works HIS Way derives directly from God's Word.

Why? **Because the Bible is the only book that truly transforms.** If you've been longing for any kind of life transformation, God's Word is the best place to find it.

This book is a collection of 100 of our favorite devotionals that first appeared in the she works His way app. Each one was written by a woman in the trenches of faith, family, and work with a heart's desire to equip you as a Christ-follower, wife, mom, friend, leader, and professional.

We are grateful to serve Jesus alongside women like you.

Rooted in HIM and rooting for YOU,

Michelle Myers
She Works HIS Way founder

1

REJOICE WITH HER

. . . .

"I would much rather spend my time praying for the woman next to me than comparing myself to the woman next to me."

Jessica Hottle

I [Jessica] was more stressed than I needed to be. I was so overwhelmed. I felt like nothing was getting done. I was frustrated that the work I was doing wasn't producing the results that I thought it would.

I was done. I was so over it.

The more I tried to do to make up for the stress, the frustration, and the feeling of being completely overwhelmed, the more I got of those feelings. More stressed. More frustrated. More overwhelmed.

My head began to hang lower and lower because the women around me seemed to be moving forward and appeared to be so in sync with God.

Surely, the social media likes these women were getting (and that I wasn't getting) meant they had to be more in sync, right? There's no way that so many people could be following her without her reaching success.

It was everything I saw that they had and I didn't have that led me down the road of more strain than my body and life could manage.

So instead of focusing on what God had given me, I focused on everything He had given her.

I began to ask myself a tough question: What inside of me stops me from rejoicing with her?

That's the problem. The enemy likes to take the good gifts you have been given by God and your own insecurities to make you feel as though it's impossible to do His work. And the thing is, we have given the enemy all that power. Ugh.

Titus 1:16 shows the truth of exactly the kind of leader I was becoming: *"They profess to know God, but they deny Him in their works."*

In this letter, Paul was writing to Titus because Titus was at Crete to help transform Creetan believers. Crete was infamous for its sin. Titus was sent there to restore order, particularly in leadership.

I was proclaiming Jesus to be my Savior, but denying His work was good in my life because I wanted and focused on what the woman next to me had. When I had this perspective, was I not denying Him with my works - the work God has specifically called me to do? I was devoting myself to a god that wasn't the faithful, gracious, and merciful God of the Word.

Do you find yourself devoting your days trying the next best thing, because the woman next to you is doing it, and not because you are called to do it?

The rest of Titus 1:16 says, *"They are detestable, disobedient, unfit for any good work."*

Here is what I know to be true and stand alongside with today: I would much rather spend my time praying for the woman next to me than comparing myself to the woman next to me.

Her gifts help and come alongside my gifts. We are not hurting each other. We are only helping each other.

It's easy for us to know the truth but it is much harder to pursue the truth in our works and daily lives with intention. But, this is our call. This is our "get to" not our "have to." If you are stressed, overwhelmed, and frustrated, then take an inventory of what your foundation is on which you are trying to build.

Lord, thank You for always revealing Yourself in ways we never expect. Thank You for the tough and tender love You have for us that allows us to grow beyond what we could ever imagine. Show us Your way in our lives today. Amen!

2

GOD IN A BOX

. . . .

"We've got to stop putting human limits on a limitless God."

Somer Phoebus

Can you be anything but fully dependent on God and in a right relationship with Him?

Let's go to God's Word first and get the answer to this question before we move on.

"Trust in the Lord with all your heart
and lean not on your own understanding;
in all your ways submit to him,
and he will make your paths straight." **- Proverbs 3:5-6**

"My flesh and my heart may fail,
but God is the strength of my heart
and my portion forever." **- Psalm 73:26**

"I lift up my eyes to the mountains—
where does my help come from?
My help comes from the Lord,
the Maker of Heaven and earth." **- Psalm 121:1-2**

Total dependence is the only level of dependence God wants from us.

I [Somer] used to really struggle with dependence, and not always because I didn't trust God, although that's what it looked like. After a lot of prayer, I realized that I was struggling because, most of the time, I truly felt like my situation wasn't big enough for Him. I would think about my neighbor down the road fighting cancer, or my friend who just tragically lost her little girl, or that other friend whose marriage was hanging on by a thread and I'd think, "Wow, that's what God needs to be dealing with, not my 'little' problems."

But this is such an absolutely absurd way to view God. And more than anything, it's a dangerous way to view God.

Another struggle is that I'm someone who can totally shut down when I feel overwhelmed. Can you relate? It's why I spend so much time coaching women in productivity and fixing what's broken in their businesses. Because when I get behind or stranded, I'm prone to just giving up. But God revealed to me how much my inability to deal with feeling overwhelmed and my view of Him were related.

You see, I was putting my human limitations on a limitless God.

I wonder what other weaknesses of my own I may be projecting on GOD?

I never struggle to remember the bigness of God! I never struggle to remember that Jesus was all man AND all God. But I do struggle to think that someone so big and who is all man + all God could care about me so deeply!

He does though.

In 1 Samuel chapter 8 we find this verse:

And the Lord said to Samuel, "Obey the voice of the people in all that they say to you, for they have not rejected you, but they have rejected me from being king over them." - 1 Samuel 8:7

God reminded Samuel that when his people all but ignored him, he was not the one who was being rejected.

And in that moment, God reminded me of how personal He was! I saw how much God cares about our feelings. He was coaching Samuel and, like the good Father He is, He reminded Samuel that what was happening wasn't his fault.

God cares about our hearts, our hurts, and our "little" things.

That's my area of struggle. That's where I can so foolishly put God in this weird much-too-small box. What about you? In what areas of your life do you do the same?

Maybe you struggle with forgiveness, so it's hard for you to understand how God can forgive you.

Maybe you struggle with greed, so generosity is difficult since you think God or your church are greedy too.

Maybe you struggle with honesty, so when you read God's Word, it's hard for you to believe that what it says is 100% truth.

Instead of turning God into a version of ourselves, let's pattern our hearts around who He has revealed Himself to be.

God, I'm sorry for the times that my human mind forgets Your greatness. Forgive me for not seeing You like the incredible, all-powerful God You are. God, help me to trust You with my life, and to fully depend on You for my every need. You're so good to comfort when I'm upset and to provide when I'm in need. Thank You, Father! I love You. Amen.

3

CHILD SACRIFICE

. . . .

"We must be proactive to ensure we are not sacrificing our kid's childhood to achieve something for ourselves."

Michelle Myers

If you've ever studied the Old Testament deeply, it doesn't take long to understand that much of it is...colorful. Vivid. Violent.

I mean, from getting devoured by a bear for making fun of Elisha's baldness (2 Kings 2) to all that was left of Queen Jezebel was her skull, her feet, and the palms of her hands (2 Kings 10), the Old Testament can be a bit uncomfortable to read at times.

But perhaps the most uncomfortable I [Michelle] am in reading the Old Testament?

2 Chronicles 28:3:

"Moreover, he burned incense in the valley of Ben-hinnom and burned his sons in fire, according to the abominations of the nations whom the Lord had driven out before the sons of Israel."

You read that correctly. This is actually referring to the common Canaanite practice of child sacrifice, which the Lord strongly condemned in Leviticus 20:1-5.

Child sacrifice was viewed as the greatest gift ancient pagan religions believed they could offer to protect themselves from evil or get back in good standing when they angered their "gods."

No doubt, the mere idea makes you sick to your stomach or even brings tears to your eyes. But let's remove the horror and allow ourselves to see the big picture of what was happening.

The pagan religions were sacrificing their children for their own gain and their own prosperity.

You see where I'm going with this, right?

Just as we cringe at the thought of young children as actual sacrifices, we should be as proactive to ensure we are not sacrificing our kid's childhood to achieve something for ourselves.

This is NOT a mom guilt trip. I repeat, this is **NOT** a mom guilt trip.

It *IS* possible to work while you're raising kids. *(There would be no place for this ministry if it weren't possible!)*

But lean in, sweet friend. Just because it's possible, that doesn't mean that it's easy. Or natural. Because it's not.

We talk all the time about our priority order around here of what connects us at *she works HIS way:*

1) God
2) Family
3) Work

It's so easy to type, but it's hard to live – because the enemy will constantly be pulling at you to live your life out of God's order.

CONSTANTLY. Daily. Sometimes, even, moment by moment.

First, let me be transparent. I don't do this perfectly. I don't always get it right. But let me get practical today and give you five guardrails I use to help me ensure that my priorities aren't just talk, they're truth.

1) Pray about it.
I don't want to rely on myself to get it right. I won't. I begin every day from a place of desperation, begging God to protect me from the enemy's schemes and to put His spirit of discernment in me.

2) Ask your kids to hold you accountable.
Depending on your kid's ages, you may have to wait on this one a while. But I've given my boys (ages 7 and 4) 100% permission to call me out if they ever feel like they've taken a backseat to work. And I never argue with their feelings. I just immediately redirect my attention to them. That way, they always know that when it comes to them, *work can wait.*

3) Apologize
It's not enough to confess and repent to God when we mess up. We must ask for forgiveness from those we've wronged. I know I'm still only seven years in to

7

being a parent, so I will never claim to be an expert. But I pray that my refusal to pretend to be a perfect parent keeps communication channels open with my kids for their entire lives.

4) Be intentional at home
We talk a lot about setting goals and being focused at work. But does your family get that same attention? If they're more important than work, then **they should**. Hold yourself accountable to the same level of "WOW" at home as you do with your clients and teammates.

5) "Opportunity" is not always good.
It's hard to say it better than John Maxwell: "Learn to say 'no' to the good so you can say 'yes' to the best." You will have many years to work and build your career when your kids are no longer under your roof. Make sure that you consider them and how quickly they grow up as you weigh career opportunities.

This will not look 100% the same for all of us as we live this out, so don't think that your life has to mirror her life to be walking in obedience to God. We're not supposed to look like one another; we're supposed to look like Him, despite our different assignments.

So let's pray. Let's be intentional. And let's cheer one another on to do more of what really matters.

I'm rooting for you.

God, help me to be the wife my husband deserves and the mom my children need. I know that sometimes productivity in parenting can be hard to measure, but God, don't let me get distracted in my pursuit of that holy and high calling of wife and mom. Protect me from being deceived. Fill me with Your discernment. Keep me on Your path for my life. I love You. Amen.

4

ACCOUNTS OF FRUIT

. . . .

"We stand on shaky ground if we care more about
getting accolades for our God-given gifts than about
the spiritual fruit in the lives of our listeners."

Emily Copeland

My husband, Colston, and I [Emily] entered full time ministry at the ages of 21
and 22 as young newlyweds. We led youth ministry, which meant that we were
only a few years older than some of our students. But even from a very early
start in vocational ministry, it didn't take long to see a side of ministry that just
didn't feel right. We would attend conferences where pastors were treated like
celebrities – untouchable and hidden from the public. We would see ministries
that spoke enthusiastically about the numbers in their audiences, but not about
the heart change that was the supposed drive behind the events.

I hope you haven't written me off as pious or condemning. I can see the
brokenness because I, too, am broken. I'm fully guilty of being addicted to the
gift of applause. In fact, when the applause of achievement as a young model
went away, I was left paralyzed with a heart that was desperate to find it again.

The truth is that the gift of applause is never safe in the hands of broken people
who use it to build the foundation of their lives.

It's no secret that Paul was a man who deserved every religious accolade that
could have been given. He was considered a "faultless Pharisee" because he was
the best that there was and he had plenty of reason to brag. But in Philippians
chapter 3 verse 8, Paul claims that all of his religious knowledge and gifting is
garbage. His only gain is Jesus Christ.

Then Paul turns the table to ensure that the Philippians know that he is grateful
for their gifts of provision for his ministry. They had sent him aid and anything
that he needed to continue spreading the gospel. He then makes a statement
that holds the key to unlocking the mess that many Christians in leadership have
found themselves in today, over decades, and even centuries.

"Not that I desire your gifts; what I desire is that more be credited to your account." Philippians 4:17

In my own translation, Paul says, "Thanks for the gifts, friends, but – gift or no gift – I am most concerned about the fruit that is in your account before God."

As women of influence, it translates for us like this: We need to be leaders who care more about the fruit being produced in our audience's lives than the number of eyes and ears that we can captivate. Are we fighting for our audience's heart or for their attention? Do we care more about what's being added to our reputation or what is being added to our listeners' accounts before God?

Because only God can see a person's heart, it's important that we as leaders are always asking ourselves honest questions without being concerned about what others perceive our motives to be:

1) Does this post/video/speaking engagement encourage my audience towards Jesus? Or does it simply grow my work/ministry?

2) Would I be willing to step out of the spotlight to focus on one-on-one discipleship if God called me to do that?

3) Can I accept that my God-given gifts can be just as influential in small settings as they can be in front of a large audience?

4) Do I trust that, since God is most concerned about a person's spiritual fruit in their account before Him, that I am responsible to make it my top priority for them too?

As we stay in our lane that God has created for us and as we fight to help our listeners develop spiritual fruit in their lives, we are left with a promise that we can lay as our strong foundation:

"And my God will meet all of your needs according to the riches of His glory in Christ Jesus." Philippians 4:19

Our need for applause: filled by Christ. Our need for accolades: filled by Christ. Our need to be seen and wanted: filled by Christ. And our joy? To see disciples emerging from under our influence with spiritual fruit baskets overflowing as God gets every ounce of the glory.

God, You alone know just how frail we are in our own strength. With one moment of applause, we can be swept away in a trance of empty accolades. But You've given us influence as working women at home and in the workplace to point others to You. Draw us in and remind us of our place in You so that we can make the most of every moment and every encounter today. We love You. Amen.

5

GOD NEVER DISAPPOINTS

. . . .

"There is nothing we can do today to make God love us more,
and nothing we might do to make Him love us less."

Liz Patton

When I [Liz] was a senior in college, I moved home to live with my parents for my final semester in order to complete my student teaching. I'll never forget the morning of my 22nd birthday. I was so excited because I was actually going to be at home for the first time in four years—with the people who birthed me—and I had big expectations for an epic birthday celebration.

And guess what? They forgot! I mean they legit forgot. (*Until later that day, and then I promise they made up for it.*) But I'll never forget how disappointed I was on the drive to school that morning. There may have even been tears. Because, I mean, who forgets their loved one's birthday?

Fast forward just about five years. I was newly married, and we were driving to the gym at crack-of-dawn early on the morning of my husband's birthday. And you guessed it—I forgot it was his birthday!!! I'm going to blame it on not having had enough coffee yet, and when I finally remembered about ten minutes into our drive, I apologized profusely. He still teases me about it because, I mean, who forgets their loved one's birthday?

Here's the thing, my sweet friends—people will always disappoint us. Always.

There is only One who will never disappoint:

"And this hope will not lead to disappointment. For we know how dearly God loves us, because he has given us the Holy Spirit to fill our hearts with his love." Romans 5:5, NLT

Oh, I love that so much; don't you?! I find such comfort in knowing that God will never disappoint us, He loves us dearly, and He has given us the Holy Spirit to fill our hearts with love! That's some good stuff right there, sister!

The other amazing thing is that even when we mess up and sin, because of God's great love for us and what Christ did for us on the cross, we will never disappoint Him! There is nothing we can do today to make God love us more, and nothing we might do to make Him love us less. He simply loves us because He loves us. That's just who He is.

I love how the late Brennan Manning described God:

"He is not moody or capricious; He knows no seasons of change. He has a single relentless stance toward us: He loves us. He is the only God that man has ever heard of who loves sinners. False gods—the gods of human manufacturing—despise sinners, but the Father of Jesus loves all, no matter what they do. But of course, this is almost too incredible for us to accept."

But when we DO accept His great love for us, it changes everything! So no matter what you do (or what others do to you), rather than feeling disappointment, let me remind you today that your Father's love for you is unconditional and never ending. He sees you, He loves you, and He will never disappoint you.

Dear God, thank You for your unconditional love for me! Thank You that even when I mess up, You still love me. Thank You that even when the people in my life disappoint me, You never will. Your love for me is the same yesterday, today, and tomorrow, and this fills my heart with so much joy! I love You forever. Amen.

FEELINGS

. . . .

"Be diligent in the place you are."

Somer Phoebus

But it doesn't feel like this is what I'm supposed to be doing…

I'm {Somer} going to get right to the point today. It's not about how we feel.

Ever.

As I grow in my walk with Christ and as a business woman I see myself praying less for what I want and more for what God wants for me.

My feelings vs. God's plan for me
My dreams vs. God's reality for me
My quick trip vs. God's extended journey

And I'm not praying that way because I've got it all figured out, but because I've learned that praying for my desires, especially in regards to calling and career, has gotten me nowhere. Actually, I take that back…a few times it has taken me backwards.

Let me clarify: I'm speaking about feelings and desires as in our fleshly feelings and desires. Once the Holy Spirit captures our hearts, He will determine our desires. But it's an everyday discipline to allow your heart to be captured. One of the first signs that you've managed to escape His grip is when you let your mind begin to feel **discontent** with where God has you and **disconnected** to your calling.

We then sometimes take those feelings of discontentment and especially disconnection and tell ourselves that they are God's doing, that He is making us feel this way because it's time to move on. That's a scary idea to bring forward.

It's really easy to feel discontent in a calling when that calling isn't treating you like you think you should be treated, or when the success that you expected has not yet come, or when nobody has a clue what you're actually putting into this calling.

I mean who wouldn't naturally begin to disconnect when you feel overworked, under-appreciated, and never rewarded? One Person:

Jesus.

He was all those things, but He never asked God for a different mission.

In this world that encourages constant change and growth, we're choosing to chase the wrong kind of growth. We should be growing in our walk with Christ, in the knowledge of our work, and in our love for people and serving others. But instead, we're growing away from those things and onto whatever the newest, shiniest opportunity is.

Growth doesn't always mean you leave things behind. It can often mean you elevate them with you!

Be the difference-maker in the place God has you.

I'm urging you today to put your feelings aside, not to make a single decision based on how you feel until you know that how you feel is an overflow of the Holy Spirit's work in your heart.

As followers of Christ we're all in ministry no matter our JOB, and ministry isn't easy. But running from it will only make things worse.

Be diligent in the place you are, friend. When/if God decides to move you, He won't need any help from you, so there's no need to push.

Dear God, please help us to pursue the right kind of growth. Teach us not to run away from the mission You've given us and help us to rest in the place where You've put us. We don't want to miss Your plan for our lives just because it doesn't look like what we think it should. We love You. Amen.

7

SERVING DEFEATED ENEMIES

. . . .

"I refuse to waste my life serving the gods of a defeated enemy."

Michelle Myers

I [Michelle] know that we warn against having false idols frequently here. Why?

First, we talk about it a lot because Scripture talks about it a lot. *(After all, it was the first commandment given of God's ten!)* And what's important to Him is important to us.

But also, we constantly revisit this topic because, in the position that you are in as a *she works HIS way* woman, you are constantly faced with worldly messages that conflict with God's way.

Every single day, a battle happens for your heart. We must know the battle is coming, and sweet friend, we don't have the option to watch the war.

We must fight.

This verse stopped me in my morning reading, and my heart sank as I realized how frequently *this* is where false idols begin:

"He [Amaziah] did right in the sight of the Lord, yet not with a whole heart."
2 Chronicles 25:2

A divided heart. Maybe you are doing right in the sight of the Lord...but does He have to share your heart with something else?

Maybe a position? A paycheck? An Instagram account? Earthly applause?

Here's the truth: When God doesn't have our whole heart, that's when we are tempted to serve other things.

Consider what happened to Amaziah. Just a few verses later, after God has helped him defeat the Edomites, he began worshiping the gods of the enemy he had just defeated. *(Read 2 Chronicles 25:14 for yourself – you can't make this stuff up!)*

And examine God's response:

Then the anger of the Lord burned against Amaziah, and He sent Him a prophet who said to him, "Why have you sought the gods of the people who have not delivered their own people from your hand?" 2 Chronicles 25:15

Let that sink in. Don't you just want to shake him and ask, "Dude, for real?! Why are you serving the gods of a defeated enemy?!"

It's easy to see when it's about bowing before statues and burning incense.

But the same is true for other gods. Money. Power. Recognition. They are pursuits of the world. They are empty.

They are gods of a defeated enemy.

I always want to include a disclaimer: If you've achieved success in your business and you've moved up in your company and received bonuses or awards, you are not necessarily wrong. Money, leadership positions, and winning awards are not bad in themselves.

Your heart just can't belong to them. Not even a part of it. Your whole heart must belong to God.

I understand the tension. I feel it myself…practically every day.

But I always come back to the real choice I have to make:

Today, I can either choose to give my energy to serving my living and active God or waste my time serving the gods of defeated enemies.

Will you pray this next simple sentence out loud with me right now?

I refuse to waste my life serving the gods of a defeated enemy.

We see it over and over in God's Word: God uses the humble. He promotes the unknown. He chooses to use us to do His work, despite our weaknesses and imperfections.

If we truly believe that He knows best and has good plans for our future *(Jeremiah 29:11)*, let's act like it. Let's give Him whole hearts and trust Him for the rest.

16

God, I really meant that prayer I said out loud to You just now. I refuse to waste my life serving the gods of a defeated enemy. Help me see when other things are battling for pieces of my heart, and give me Your strength to fight to be fully Yours. Convict me often. I trust whatever You want to do with my life. I'm ready, and I'm willing. I love You. Amen.

8

BECOME > DO

. . . .

"He's not just looking at what you do.
He's watching who you are becoming."

Jessica Hottle

Our actions can make others want to give praise to the Father.

So, no matter what we do, in the end, it's never about us.

Therefore, when we look to be admired *(or approved)* by others, we lose the reward of the Father.

Like C.S. Lewis said, this is not about thinking less of ourselves, but about thinking of ourselves less.

But, our actions only begin to change when our hearts change first.

I [Jessica] wrote this in my journal the other day: "When you claim nothing as yours, everything will be given to you." Those words were based on the footnotes in my Bible as I began reading through The Beatitudes in Matthew 5:3-11.

When you read through the Beatitudes it doesn't say, "When you work hard, money comes to you." Or, "The more followers you gain, the more successful you will be."

The problem is, that's where 90% of our focus goes – on building our own kingdom here on earth.

We have become "too busy" to do the real work, the heart work. The work that matters to God the most. He's not just looking at what you do. He's watching who you are becoming.

Here are a few of my favorites from the Beatitudes in Matthew 5:

"What wealth is offered to you when you feel your spiritual poverty! For there is no charge to enter the realm of heaven's kingdom." (v.3)

"How enriched you are when you crave righteousness! For you will be surrounded with fruitfulness." (v. 6)

"What bliss you experience when your heart is pure! For then your eyes will open to see more and more of God." (v.8)

We gain so much more when our focus is on becoming rather than doing.

It's why I stated earlier that our actions will lead others to give praise to the Father (Matthew 5:15-16). Remember the saying: "People won't necessarily remember what you do but they will remember how you made them feel"?

Ask your heart today: Who are you becoming? What do you crave? What are you seeking? Is your heart pure?

Father, my heart is leaning into Yours today. Let whatever is on my heart be revealed to me. The good. The bad. The ugly. Father, refocus my attention not on what I am doing, but on who I am becoming. I'm ready for it. I love You! Amen!

9

"YOU'RE A HITTER, KID!"

. . . .

"What if instead of judging others, we loved on them like Jesus and called forth in them who they are becoming?"

Liz Patton

When our son first started playing Little League baseball, his coach yelled something to him when he got up to bat for the very first time that I [Liz] will never forget. He yelled, "You're a hitter, Kid!"

And you know what? Our kid believed him. He became a hitter.

Imagine what we could accomplish if we had more belief in what God could make us become and do through us. And, even more importantly, imagine what the people in our lives could become if we called out in them what they are becoming!

I have to confess that I'm not always great at this. In fact, I can tend to be judgmental of others. It's a quality that I'm not proud of and something that I often need to confess. Maybe you can relate? *(And maybe right now you are judging me for being judgmental! LOL!)*

I was recently reading, *Everybody Always* by Bob Goff and something he said convicted me and stopped me dead in my tracks. He said, "When we make ourselves the hall-monitor of other people's behavior, we risk having approval become more important than Jesus' love."

Ouch, right?!

We are even reminded about the danger of passing judgment in **Matthew 7:1-2: "Do not judge, or you too will be judged. For in the same way you judge others, you will be judged, and with the measure you use, it will be measured to you."**

Here's the thing...we don't need to approve of others to love them. What if instead of judging others, we loved on them like Jesus and called out in them who God has created them to be and who He says they are becoming?!

You're a great wife and mom, Kid!
You're an amazing entrepreneur, Kid!
You're a business owner, Kid!
You're a leader, Kid!
You're an athlete, Kid!
You're a disciple-maker, Kid!
You're an inspiration, Kid!
You're an encourager, Kid!
You're a world-changer, Kid!

God did this over and over again in the Bible. He told Moses he was a leader, and Moses became one. He told Noah he was the captain of his ship and would keep animals and humanity alive, and Noah did. He told Sarah she was a mother, and she became one. He told Paul *(who at the time was persecuting the Lord's disciples)* that he would carry His name, and Paul became an instrument to bear Jesus' name to the Gentiles.

My sweet sisters, today instead of being Hall Monitors who give away judgment, let's be Jesus Lovers who give away grace and encouragement. Let's call people according to who they are becoming!

"Let each of us please his neighbor for his good, to build him up." Romans 15:2

Dear God, forgive me for all of the times I've passed judgment on others. Help me be an encourager to others. Help me to see them with Your eyes and to love them with Your heart. I want to call out in them who they are becoming, just like You have called me. I love You. Amen.

10

FALSE ADVERTISING

. . . .

"We can't play the role for very long before we become too weary of 'keeping up' with what we are speaking about but not acting on."

Emily Copeland

I [Emily] recently purchased a piece of wall art that was a large canvas scroll with a beautiful quote on it. There is a perfect spot for it in our entryway, so I spent the money. I envisioned that this sign would encourage and inspire us by its words and that it would really brighten up the space.

As soon as I received it in the mail, I was instantly deflated. This beautiful piece of canvas turned out to be one big sheet of computer paper (my definition) and it was crinkled from top to bottom. It wasn't at all what it was advertised to be, and now the painful process of returns and refunds began.

When I was reading Mark 11 and the story about Jesus and the fig tree, I immediately thought of my sign that was essentially an experience with false advertising.

Here's what happened: Jesus and the disciples were leaving Bethany and Jesus was very hungry. He saw a fig tree off in the distance, which was recognizable by its leaves, and headed over to it. As he reached up, he noted that there were many leaves, but there was no fruit. The leaves were false advertising because this tree professed to having fruit, but did not actually bear fruit and was therefore a useless fig tree. (Mark 11:13)

"Then he (Jesus) said to the tree, 'May no one ever eat fruit from you again.' And his disciples heard him say it." Mark 11:14

Jesus cursed the tree. But He didn't curse the tree because it didn't have fruit, he cursed the tree because it had leaves that gave the false advertisement of fruit.

So if Jesus cursed a fruit-less tree for false advertisement, how should He respond if there is any part of our lives that gives a false advertisement to our walk with God or our love for other people?

God cannot work through a life that is all talk and no walk. We will be known by our fruit, not by how well we can communicate our relationship with Jesus. We will be known by our fruit, not by how attractive our life looks. We will be known by our fruit, not by how many people approve of what we say.

Because the Holy Spirit is actively working in our lives as believers, we will not be blinded to any areas of our lives that may be false advertisement if we seek Him on the matter. And friends, we can't play the role for very long before we become too weary of "keeping up" with what we are speaking about but not acting on.

False advertisement in any way is crippling to us and damaging to those around us. So, it's better for us to step out of the spotlight and get it together with God than to continue presenting truth on a foundation made of sand.

This is a heart-check for every Christian woman! No one is exempt. Let's lean into our accountability people and make the time that it takes to bear fruit through an authentic and surrendered walk with Him.

God, this very short snippet of Scripture holds a lot of weight for us. As Jesus revealed the harsh reality of false advertisement, it also gives us hope that a life full of fruit can have the opposite effect: major Kingdom impact! Stir our souls to know where we may be getting this wrong. Walk with us as we seek You first! We love You. Amen.

11

YOU ARE DIFFERENT THAN HER

. . . .

*"The woman standing next to you should always
be an inspiration but not the influence."*

Jessica Hottle

Fact: The way the Lord is going to bless you, raise you up, and speak to you will look different than the woman standing next to you.

But, for many, when we see the woman next to us moving forward, "succeeding", then we begin to think that whatever she did to get where she is going, we must do too.

The woman standing next to you should always be an inspiration but not the influence.

Looking at the woman next to us as an inspiration gives us encouragement. It allows God to be the sole influence over our lives because we see the work He is doing in hers.

If we look at the woman next to us as the main influence, then most of what we do next will involve us copying her to try to get her results.

It just won't work.

I [Jessica] have been reading in the book of Matthew lately. If God wanted to do everything the same way.

Yet, He doesn't.

He loves the personal connection with you. The way He made you to think. How He created you to grow. And, more importantly, how you choose to love Him.

I just love the way Jesus never really heals the same way twice. He heals differently every time and with different words and actions.

Some with simple words. (See Matthew 9:2)
Some with a gentle touch. (See Matthew 8:3)
Some simply by their faith. (See Matthew 8:8-10)

What I want us to acknowledge is that those who came to Jesus for healing all had different backgrounds, stories, and ways they lived their lives. Each situation that Jesus encountered was specific to that person's story, belief, and life.

Your business/ministry, my friend, is going to look so different from hers, from the way it works out to the way that God shows up.

I'll end with this question: Can we both agree that hers is just as important as yours?

Father, I'm so thankful for the way that You love me, the way that You show up in my life, and the way You are quick to forgive me when I get it wrong. You are my first influence and guide. Lead me to where You want me to go. I love You! In Jesus name, Amen!

12

NOT ALWAYS BAD, BUT NEVER BEST

. . . .

"We are not called to the world's standards; but to God's."

Michelle Myers

"Hey, you do a lot with Christian women who work, right?"

I [Michelle] received this text message yesterday from a college friend I don't see often. When I told her I did, her second text said this:

"Okay, so explain to me why so many women who claim Christ have to tell me how much money they make all the time. It is all over my news-feed..."

And this is just the most recent account. It's probably one of the most common work-related conversations I have with believers outside of the business world.

So today, let's talk about a question I'm asked often: As a believer, should I share my income success?

Good news: The Bible isn't silent about this. Let's use His answer as our foundation:

"Thus says the Lord, 'Let not a wise man boast of his wisdom, and let not the mighty man boast of his might, let not a rich man boast of his riches; but let him who boasts boast of this, that he understands and knows Me, that I am the Lord who exercises loving-kindness, justice and righteousness on earth; for I delight in these things,' declares the Lord." Jeremiah 9:23-24

Two things immediately jumped out to me:

Being wise, mighty, or rich may not always be bad, but it will never be best.

As Christ-followers, we are to be delighted by the things that delight God. These verses highlight that God delights when we understand and know Him.

God distinguishes between *being* wise, mighty, or rich and *talking* about being wise, mighty or rich.

It's not that He's ashamed of our wisdom, power, or riches, but these verses contain specific instructions not to boast in them. And we know our disobedience does not please God.

But it doesn't stop there; it goes deeper. Because the reality is, boasting reveals what we value. Boasting reveals what we want others to know about us.

And anytime we boast in ourselves, we miss an opportunity to share the most important thing about us: Not anything we've done, but what God has done for us.

So let's cut to the heart and examine our motives:

Even if you don't boast out loud in your accomplishments, whether income or anything else, what do you long to be admired for?

And let's not just give the "right" answer.
- What consumes your thoughts?
- What gets your consistent effort?
- Do you *really* trust God with your success?
- If all "perks" of what you do were stripped away, would anything be left?
- Are you willing to obey God's instruction over industry standards?

Ultimately, the reality is that your heart and motives are between you and God alone. Regardless of how we may be able to manipulate, spin, or justify our words and actions, nothing is hidden from Him.

What I think doesn't matter. What you think doesn't matter. What he/she thinks doesn't matter.

But what God ***knows***, does matter.

God, our thoughts, words, actions, and motives are easy to manipulate, spin, and justify. But nothing is hidden from You. And You are not silent about business issues that have become industry standards. Help us remember that we are not called to the world's standard, but we are called to Yours. Hold us accountable to live like it. Convict us when we fall short. Right now, I commit to Your instruction, regardless of whether or not it aligns with my thoughts. I love You and I trust You. Amen.

13

THE COMEBACK

. . . .

"You don't become unworthy of the mission because of your failures.
You become proof of God's goodness and His ability to take
broken people and use them for His glory."

Emily Copeland

I [Emily] had a close friend of mine tell me this week that she felt like she needed a comeback. She felt as though she had moved away from God and that she was lacking a lot of peace. Not because she had messed up in a big way, but through a lot of small decisions that didn't include God in them, she became distant and just needed a fresh start with Him.

Have you felt this way too? Maybe you have experienced making a really big mistake or maybe you've recently spent time away from God's Word and neglecting time in prayer. Maybe you've been hurt and can't get past the hurdle of the pain.

Can I encourage you today? I want to show you the pattern of one of the most well-known Jesus-followers of all time and how he made a comeback that has echoed through the centuries.

Just look at Peter. The man who's greatest failure has been read by billions of people. He was one of Jesus' first disciples and, in the end, one who was faithful to Jesus even unto death.

Peter followed and served God wholeheartedly from the very beginning. He went all in. He got to witness some of the greatest miracles first-hand and he got to be with Jesus in many of the most intimate moments of teaching.

But, when it came time for Jesus' death, something wild (and eerily familiar to us) came over him: Fear. People who were angry enough to kill Jesus asked Peter if he knew Jesus. And Peter said 'no' (John 18).

Then, we see Jesus' heart in John 21 when He reinstates Peter to the mission. The moment is overflowing with forgiveness, restoration, unconditional love. Jesus gives him the mission: "Feed my lambs" (v. 15).

Finally, after Jesus goes back to Heaven, we see Peter take on his mission with zero fear and a mountain of boldness. This is my personal favorite section of Scripture when it comes to Peter! We see Peter step into his role from God with more courage than ever before. He was in his sweet spot. Not because he was good at his job (sharing the gospel), but because he was a man forgiven of his failures and commissioned to represent Jesus. That was his fire!

Peter proclaimed to the unbelieving crowd, ***"Therefore let all Israel be assured of this: God has made this Jesus, whom you crucified, both Lord and Messiah." Acts 2:36***

"Those who accepted his message were baptized, and about 3,000 were added to their number that day." Acts 2:41

Ultimately, Peter's story is not about his failure. Peter's story is about the goodness of Jesus Christ to overcome any sin and any mistake when we seek Him. And girls, our stories are no different. You are not the hero of your own story – Jesus is. You are not the driving force behind the Kingdom work you've been given – Jesus is. Which means that your failure will never be (and has never been) final.

Listen. You don't become unworthy of the mission because of your failures. You become proof of God's goodness and His ability to take broken people and use them for His glory.

Your comeback is this: Repent, seek His face every day, and step into the position that God has given you without holding back. Today is the day and people are waiting!

God, everything about our life is designed to bring You glory. Even our mistakes can mark our story forever as the moment that You rescued us and then continued to run with us on our mission. Help us to let go of doubts, fears, shame, and guilt today. Thank You for never giving up on us. We love You! Amen.

14

LIVING UP TO YOUR NAME

. . . .

"There's no need to wrestle! Just rest!"

Somer Phoebus

I [Somer] LOVE the story of Jacob wrestling with God. I wish I could say it's only because it's a great story, but unfortunately I think it's probably because I can relate so much to the struggle for control. Of all the pain points I hear about from other females (believers or not), control is probably in the top three.

Why do we think we can control things?

Jacob was willing to fight all night because he couldn't imagine giving anyone else the control. Have you ever been there? There's a word for it: Pride. Pride is a sneaky sin issue to have. It can disguise itself in many different ways, like confidence, self-care, independence, etc. But pride is really a lack of trust in God. And when it's present, it will affect every aspect of your life!

"The same night he arose and took his two wives, his two female servants, and his eleven children, and crossed the ford of the Jabbok. He took them and sent them across the stream, and everything else that he had. And Jacob was left alone. And a man wrestled with him until the breaking of the day. When the man saw that he did not prevail against Jacob, he touched his hip socket, and Jacob's hip was put out of joint as he wrestled with him. Then he said, "Let me go, for the day has broken." But Jacob said, "I will not let you go unless you bless me." And he said to him, "What is your name?" And he said, "Jacob." Then he said, "Your name shall no longer be called Jacob, but Israel, for you have striven with God and with men, and have prevailed." Then Jacob asked him, "Please tell me your name." But he said, "Why is it that you ask my name?" And there he blessed him. So Jacob called the name of the place Peniel, saying, "For I have seen God face to face, and yet my life has been delivered." The sun rose upon him as he passed Penuel, limping because of his hip." Genesis 32:22-31

I've read this passage multiple times, but one night, when I heard verse 28, it especially stuck with me.

Jacob's name meant "cheater." Literally, his parents named him "cheater." Can you imagine? I've heard some bad names in my lifetime, some that made me wonder what in the world that person's parents were thinking, but to call your child "cheater?" That's low.

What is so sad though is that Jacob lived down to that name. He actually was what we would call in our day, a pretty big jerk. For example, he cheated his brother out of his own inheritance and stole his God-given blessing.

Jacob had lived with his awful name his whole life, when suddenly, after this wrestling match with God, he receives a new name. God calls him "Israel", which means Warrior Prince!

So from Cheater to Warrior Prince.

I would say that's a pretty enormous upgrade.

It made me wonder though, what would God call me? Am I living to the potential of "Somer" when He wants me to be a warrior princess?

Am I so obsessed with being in control that I'm willing to wrestle God for it? All along KNOWING that I won't win? Because I do know that I won't win. And I would bet that you do too.

Are there times when you can't see God because you're in your own way? If so, then get out of the way, friend!

God is so good! He wants good for us but we have to trust Him! We have to give up and lose the wrestling match in order to WIN.

There's no need to wrestle. Just rest. God's got you!

What do you say we live the kind of life that would warrant God giving us a crazy awesome name like Warrior Princess! Deal?

God, I love You! I want You to have all control of my life. Because I struggle with that, God, please show me the moment I start to try to pull things back in my own hands. God, help me see the mistake before I make it! I surrender my life to You. Use me as You see fit! Amen.

15

CHRIST-LIKE

. . . .

*"We aren't called to be like our Christian sisters;
we are called to be like Christ."*

Liz Patton

Today I [Liz] want to dive right in and talk about the elephant in the Christian woman's proverbial living room. To be honest, I kind of argued with God when He whispered to my spirit to address this topic. So, out of obedience to Him, here goes!

As *she works His way* women, we all know better than to compare ourselves to other women's success, clothes, homes, and influence. However, if we are really honest with ourselves, one thing that trips us up in the comparison trap is measuring our spiritual lives with those of our fellow Christian sisters.

You know what I mean - we hear her talk about her amazing quiet time, and we feel like we come up short. We see her beautifully highlighted Bible, and we feel inadequate. We notice the many Bible studies she leads, and we're embarrassed that it stirs up jealousy inside of us.

If you can relate in the slightest, please hear me, sweet girl: We aren't called to be like our Christian sisters. We are called to be like Christ.

"Be perfect, therefore, as your heavenly Father is perfect." Matthew 5:48

Now before you start fretting over that word "perfect," let's look at this verse in The Message translation:

"In a word, what I'm saying is, grow up. You're kingdom subjects. Now live like it. Live out your God-created identity. Live generously and graciously toward others, the way God lives toward you."

Did you catch that? We are to live out our God-created identity! We are Kingdom subjects and are called to live like it! And I've learned that it's so much easier for me to live like it when I'm spending time with my Father. *(If you're a parent, you know your children become more like you by spending TIME with you!)*

If your relationship with your Savior is feeling a bit stale right now, here are a few things that have helped me draw near to Him when I've felt separated from Him in the past:

- Give Him your best and your first by spending time with Him before you spend time with the rest of the world. For me, that means time with God and in His Word before my face is in my phone!
- Read a version of the Bible that excites you and speaks to your soul! (Just keeping it real here, but I get lost in the "thees" and "thous" of the King James Version. I personally love NIV, ESV, and The Message!)
- Switch up your routine! If you usually start with reading your Bible and then end in prayer, try starting with prayer and then dive into His Word next. Variety is the spice of life!
- Speaking of prayer, I have found that I feel closest to Him when I'm kneeling, picturing myself at His literal feet. Maybe for you it's walking and talking with Him in nature. However you feel closest to Him, cultivate that.
- Play worship music. I love putting my ear buds in (since my family is still asleep) and using that time to enter into His presence.
- Get plugged into your local church. Join a Bible study. Surround yourself with other women who are holding you accountable to run hard after Him.
- Take notes during the weekly sermons. Ever since doing this, I'm able to reflect on the sermon during the week, dive into the Scriptures more thoroughly, and not just listen, but actually apply what our pastor is teaching.

And please don't misunderstand me—I don't share any of these tips because I feel as though I have it all figured out! I have leaned into these practices out of a place of desperation, a place when I felt far from God. And He has used those strategies to woo me back to Him—He's SO good like that!

He loves you, He sees you, and He's waiting for you! I want to leave you with this final Scripture from Galatians 6:4-5:

"Make a careful exploration of who you are and the work you have been given, and then sink yourself into that. Don't be impressed with yourself. Don't compare yourself with others. Each of you must take responsibility for doing the creative best you can with your own life."

Dear God, I love You. I want to feel Your presence in a real and mighty way today. Woo me to You. Draw me to You. As I spend time with You, may our time together change me and shape me into the woman You've created me to be. Help me hunger for Your Word and help me thirst for time spent with You in the quiet places that are reserved for just You and me. Amen.

16

HEAVENLY RESOURCES

. . . .

"We can't rely on earthly resources to do a heaven-sized job."

Emily Copeland

Have you ever given someone a gift only to find out shortly after that they lost it? I [Emily] just recently found out this happened to a close friend. My initial reaction was frustration because let's be real, it feels like wasted money, right? But also, that friend will not get to experience the joy of the gift and all of the wonderful things I had planned for it! (Yes, I've now realized that the gift may have been more for my pleasure than for theirs!)

It is such a simple example that does not do justice to the passage I'm about to share with you, but I wanted to get your mind familiar with the sting of a gift given in vain.

"As God's co-workers, we urge you not to receive God's grace in vain..."
2 Corinthians 6:1-2.

Wait, can God's gift of grace really be given or received in vain? Just like the gift that I gave to my friend, the gift of grace can be received and then totally neglected. It's happened in my own life; I've received God's perfect grace and then have become passive and quiet in sharing it. I have also received God's perfect grace and then turned it around to claim the fame and the accolades of it for myself.

The term "in vain" literally means to become useless. Can you imagine the grace that God has extended to our broken and frail lives becoming useless once it's in our hands? Because I've been wrestling with this in my own personal walk, I wanted to share two important things with you that are vital to our mission of taking God's grace which we didn't deserve and allowing Him to use that grace to transform others around us.

First, just like Paul says, we are "co-workers" with God in the faith. We are not His employees, robots, or His free labor, all of which typically creates a spirit of obligation or duty. Often, if we view ourselves as just employees in the Kingdom, then grace becomes less valuable to us and we can easily neglect its worth in our life and to our mission.

Again, we are partners with God in the faith which means that we don't have the choice or luxury to become passive or quiet if we wish to experience all that God has designed for us.

Second, as co-workers, we have been given grace, but we've also been given heavenly resources to ensure that we have everything we need for the job at hand. We can't rely on earthly resources to do a Heaven-sized job. Earthly resources that we turn to most often include things like fame (being seen by others and building a platform that serves our own interest), power (controlling the plan), and riches (building our own kingdom).

But heavenly resources, such as power given from the Holy Spirit, prayer (which is direct access to the throne of God), supernatural love, and God's Word, equip us to receive God's grace and to use it as His partner to reach the lost world around us.

It should bother us when a day, week, or month goes by and we've neglected God's grace by becoming silent or too distracted to share it. Paul goes on to say,

"I tell you, now is the time of God's favor, now is the day of salvation."
2 Corinthians 6:2

Now is the time for us to get this right. Today matters more than any other day. If we've neglected God's grace and become stale in our faith, then step into the grace you've been given and rise up!

Sister, you are fully equipped with heavenly resources as God's co-worker, all because of His incredible gift of grace. Receive it, then share it. This is the privilege of your life!

God, who are we that You would make us Your co-workers in the mission of eternity? You've chosen us, given us grace to fill every crack of our lives, and gifted us with heavenly resources to which earthly resources cannot compare. Give us fresh eyes to Your grace today. We love You! Amen.

17

SHOW ME YOUR GLORY
. . . .

"Moses prayed, 'Show me YOUR glory.'
He didn't pray, 'show me my glory!'"

Michelle Myers

You can exaggerate your success in business.

You can only post pictures of your children being well-behaved and perfect.

You can pretend you know things that you don't...or have things that you don't.

And you can also pretend to have a solid walk with the Lord...when in reality, you feel empty and disconnected from your Creator.

But as long as you've got the open Bible flat and can search for Bible verses on Pinterest, you can fool a lot of people about where you are spiritually.

However, we can't fool God. And honestly, you can't fool people who are genuinely walking with the Lord, either.

Recently, there's been a book circulating among Christian women and getting a lot of attention. It's a message that sounds so good to hear, and it has "just enough Jesus" thrown in to deceive.

I'm not going to tell you what book it is. That's not the point. But I will tell you that if you're reading your Bible and if you ever open this book, you will easily be able to spot the twisted truths.

But the opposite is also true: If you're not opening your Bible, you could easily be deceived by its words.

I'm [Michelle] burdened for this increasingly post-modern Christian world that we are living in. A world that says, "I can have all I want of Jesus...until it gets hard, uncomfortable, or I don't understand. Then, I have the freedom to choose my own way."

No.

No.

NO!

Ladies, I'm going to be uncomfortably honest today. I believe there are some of us who are looking to be *she works HIS way* women because we think there's something in it for us.

We think that if we do something for God, that He will somehow owe us something in return.

We think that if we say our businesses are for Him, that He owes us better opportunities and more blessings.

I have read these words over and over again this year since I read them in January:

"And the Lord said to Moses, 'I will do the very thing you have asked, because I am pleased with you and I know you by name.' Then Moses said, "Now show me Your glory." Exodus 33:17-18

God was pleased with Moses. He knew him by name.

But notice what Moses didn't do. He didn't say, "Yeah, that's right You do. Now show me what's in it for me."

He said, "Show me YOUR glory." He didn't say, "Show me MY glory."

Friends, if we really want to see God do the miraculous in our lives and in our businesses, we can't make a shred of what we do about us. It has to be about Him. ONLY Him.

He will provide all of your needs. He will promote you and use you in places you could never get on your own.

But those opportunities FROM HIM only come when He knows you don't want any of the glory for yourself.

You're talented. You could probably get pretty far on your own. But no matter how gifted you are, you have limits that He doesn't.

Don't settle for less than what He's capable of doing through you.

May your heart cry be: Show me YOUR glory, Lord.

God, I confess that it's difficult to navigate the calling of being a light for You in the business world. I'm never going to get it right 100% of the time, and I'm so grateful for Your grace when I miss the mark. But God, I don't want to miss what You have for me here on this earth because I'm focused on my own comfort and my own desires. Rid my mind of thoughts of my own glory, and show me Your glory alone, Lord. I love You. Amen.

18

UNITY

. . . .

"Selfishness was not a part of their community,
for they shared everything they had with one another."
Acts 5:32

Jessica Hottle

"All the believers were one in mind and heart." That's what Luke wrote in **Acts 5:32**. What were Luke's next words in verse 32? *"Selfishness was not a part of their community, for they shared everything they had with one another."*

Let's back up a little bit so you can have some context.

Luke is sharing about the powerful preaching that Peter and John had been doing since Jesus ascended into Heaven. Jesus appeared to them many times in the forty days after His resurrection.

We read about Peter and John standing up and speaking boldly to the ones who persecuted Jesus and 3,000 people (and counting) were being saved every time Peter and John got up to speak. (See Acts 4:13)

We read about how they would stand up boldly but then, in the next chapter or so, Luke writes about an imprisonment they faced.

Here's the deal: Praise was on their lips, and together they stood in unity whenever persecution came their way. Not just Peter and John standing in unity, but also the other believers.

Peter and John may have been in the spotlight, but the other believers were just as significant, even if we don't know their names - because He does.

"When the believers heard their report, they raised their hands in unity, and prayed." **Acts 4:24**

"And the believers were wonderfully united as they met regularly in the temple courts in the area known as Solomon's Porch." Acts 5:13

When I [Jessica] was reading all of this in Acts, I couldn't help but to think of the Narrow Conference put on by *she works His way*.

The unity.
The togetherness.
The oneness in mind and heart.
The selfishness that is not a part of this community.

Being a *she works His way* woman doesn't come without the weight of persecution. If Jesus faced it, we will too.

We will be questioned and we will be misunderstood.

But, being at Narrow?

Praise was on our lips. In unity we stood alongside each other as we grabbed hands to pray. We experienced togetherness as we all shared the same mission, making Jesus the point of the story and our businesses. We met together in one room to worship, sing, learn, and pray.

What happened at Narrow last year is what I see happening at the beginning of Acts. We all face our own persecutions, but we stood tall together, boldly declaring the One who made it all happen.

Let me pray for your business and heart today:

Father, I lift up my sister in Christ who may feel like she is doing all kinds of work behind the scenes but not feeling noticed. Send her a reminder today that she is noticed and seen by You. I pray that You take her work and multiply it. I pray that the persecution she faces comes back as a double portion of blessing.

I'm standing in unity with you, my friend. Praying for you!

P.S. I hope to see you at the next Narrow conference.

19

NEGOTIATIONS

· ·

"Why in the world would I ever want an all-knowing God to compromise with an unknowing me?"

Somer Phoebus

Are you a natural negotiator?

In business, it's an incredible skill to have.

In our relationships with God, not so much.

In my own walk with the Lord, I [Somer] have noticed my tendency to negotiate with my Father.

Before we go any further, we need to recognize that there are examples in Scripture where people bargained with God, and at times, it worked out. For example, in Numbers 21, Israel told God if He delivered the Canaanites into their hands, they would destroy the Canaanites' cities. God did, in fact, deliver the Canaanites to Israel, and Israel destroyed them as they promised they would.

So what is the difference between a negotiation that God would honor and one that He wouldn't?

The reason for the negotiating. If your negotiation involves an excuse of any kind, you may want to back out of that conversation quickly.

For example, these are negotiations with excuses:

"God, I would love to be able to host all of my neighbors for dinner, but our house is too small. I'm gonna need you to provide me with more space so that I can."

Or...

"God, I know I need to study Your Word on a deeper level, but right now my mornings are slammed at work, so I'm going to keep doing what I've always done until you take care of this load I'm carrying."

See the difference? Israel wanted what was best for the Kingdom of God, but negotiations like those above want what's best for **SELF**.

When we negotiate, we miss out. Negotiation is all about compromise. And if I really think about it, why in the world would I ever want an all-knowing God to compromise with an unknowing me?

So if you're like me, here are two ways I'm working on this behavior to ensure that it stops:

1. Don't allow yourself to make excuses to God.

"I tell you, on the day of judgment people will give account for every careless word they speak." **Matthew 12:36**

When we're making excuses to God, we're being careless in our conversation with Him. Thinking that we are in a place where we can bargain with Him means we have forgotten who He is and who we are in comparison. If you want something, ask for it. Matthew 21:22, 1 John 5:14, and John 14:13 teach us that asking is far more effective than negotiating.

2. Don't just seek His hands, seek His presence.

"Seek the Lord and his strength; seek his presence continuously." **Psalm 105:4**

When we are focused on ourselves more than our God, we will want things that we don't need. We will become less motivated by His love and more motivated by His blessings. God's blessings are like no other and I'm not arguing that they aren't so sweet. But His presence in our lives is better than any gift He could give. If you had nothing but Him, would it be enough? If not, you need to do some heart searching. We are much less likely to negotiate when we're content.

Let's commit to seeing God as the authority in our life, as the One that has a plan for us that doesn't need to be altered or edited!

Less negotiating, more obeying.
Less of my ideas, more of His plan.
Less making excuses, more accountability.

God, I'm sorry that I ever assume I have a better plan. God, forgive me for making excuses or trying to negotiate for my way. Please show me how to be better in my obedience and give me a heart to seek YOU and not just Your blessings. I love You so much, Lord. Amen.

20

COUNTING CATASTROPHE

. . . .

"If we want to experience true peace, we need to
put our trust in God, not numbers."

Liz Patton

Have you ever found yourself getting caught up in numbers? I [Liz] am admittedly NOT a numbers girl. In fact, I took the bare minimum math requirements in both high school and college in order to get by *(just keeping it real here, friends!)*.

But, I have to admit that I occasionally find myself getting wrapped up in numbers. Even basing my success on numbers—the number of social media followers I have, the number of people who attend my group exercise class, the number of women who sign up for our women's Bible study, the number of clients I serve, the number of miles I can run, blah, blah, blah.

This whole numbers thing really struck me while reading about David counting his fighting men in 2 Samuel 24:2:

"So the king said to Joab, the commander of the army, who was with him, 'Go through all the tribes of Israel, from Dan to Beersheba, and number the people, that I may know the number of the people.'"

You might be asking yourself, like I did when I first read this, "What's the big deal with David counting his men?"

The big deal is that his motive was pride. He wanted to see how big and impressive his kingdom really was. The counting of his soldiers was giving him worth. He was finding his identity in the size of his kingdom, not in the eyes of his God.

Ouch. The truth is, if we want to experience true peace, we need to put our trust in God alone, not in numbers.

But stay with me, because this is where it gets so good and where David sets such a wonderful example for those of us who try to find value in our "counting."

After nine months and 20 days, Joab returns with the census report. After he gives the impressive numbers to David, it says in 2 Samuel 24:10:

"David was conscience-stricken after he had counted the fighting men, and he said to the Lord, 'I have sinned greatly in what I have done. Now, O Lord, I beg you, take away the guilt of your servant. I have done a very foolish thing.'"

I love that David didn't waste any time. He didn't need to think about it, mull over it, or question if what he did was sinful. He know immediately that it was foolish and went to the Lord to ask for forgiveness right away. We need to do the same thing when we mess up! We need to own it, repent, and ask God to forgive us.

If you continue reading in this chapter, you'll learn that God gives David three options for his punishment: three years of famine, three months of being pursued by enemies, or three days of a plague. (*"Ummm...are you sure you can't offer a 4th choice, Lord?"* I would have asked!)

"David said to Gad, 'I am in deep distress. Let us fall into the hands of the Lord, for his mercy is great; but do not let me fall into the hands of men." **2 Samuel 24:14**

Wow. David, who had previously experienced both the wrath of man and God, knew that even in God's anger, He was more merciful than man! And he was exactly right because before the three days of the plague were over, *"...the Lord was grieved because of the calamity and said to the angel who was afflicting the people, 'Enough! Withdraw your hand.'"* **2 Samuel 24:16**

Oh what a merciful, loving God we serve! Doesn't it just touch your heart to picture God grieving over the suffering of His people? If we want to experience grace, we need to put ourselves in the hands of God. He is faithful.

"If we confess our sins, he is faithful and just and will forgive us our sins and purify us from all unrighteousness." **1 John 1:9**

And God's faithfulness and forgiveness, my sweet friends, is something worth counting on!

Dear God, You are so, so good to us. We are so undeserving of Your mercy and grace, and yet You so lovingly pour it out to us. Thank You! Forgive us for the times when we have allowed numbers to give us worth and value. Forgive us when we've allowed our success to seem more important than our relationship with You. Our worth is found in You alone. We love You and choose You. Amen.

21

FEAR OF GOD

. . . .

"Proper fear of God changes our improper fear of man."
- Beth Moore

Emily Copeland

Proper fear of God gave Abraham the strength to tie together the hands of his only son Isaac as he helped him up onto the altar. (Gen. 22:1-19)

Proper fear of God gave a teenage virgin the strength to trust the plan of carrying an unplanned baby and to humbly lie down in a stable to bring Him into the world. (Luke 2)

Proper fear of God may mean putting our current dreams on hold to invest in the future of our children or a ministry. Proper fear of God may mean living paycheck to paycheck while remaining obedient to the "less-exciting" calling God has placed on you. Proper fear of God may mean going the extra mile to love the person at work who mocks and ridicules you.

But proper fear of God always results in obedience, trust, and worship. Are you experiencing these in your life?

"Proper" fear of God means understanding that God began fixing man's sin problem the moment that the Garden heard that juicy bite of the forbidden fruit. In this, God has shown His loyalty to our hearts, His sovereignty over our purpose, and His justice out of His love for us. Knowing this and choosing God is what creates "proper" fear.

Ultimately, the fear of God begins with respect and ends with worship and awe. In between, we'll find obedience to His Word, and commitment to the seasons and opportunities that He has called us to.

Therefore let us be grateful for receiving a kingdom that cannot be shaken, and thus let us offer to God acceptable worship, with reverence and awe, for our God is a consuming fire. Hebrews 12:28-29

What I'm afraid of, though, as I look around and take inventory in my [Emily] own life, is that we tend to fear men and women more than we fear God.

When was the last time that God called you to do something and you didn't think about what other people would think at all? Yeah, I couldn't recall a time either. When was the last time that you chose the sidelines of God's game plan because it wouldn't make sense to the world around you? Guilty here too.

Improper fear of man (caring more about the opinions of man) leads us to question the heart of God which may be one of the most dangerous places for us to be. We think, "It doesn't seem logical", but what we are really saying is, "God, I don't believe that you've taken all of the parts of this into account." Or, "People would think that I'm a lunatic", which really just translates to, "God, you don't have my best interest in mind because I would look like a fool."

Friends, we do not belong to a club of do-gooders who do what they please when they please, call it charity, and add a gold star to their wall. We are women who have been given a Hand-Designed calling and a Kingdom-sized purpose that comes with the privilege to take our Creator at His Word and to worship Him with every ounce of our lives! Fearing God means that we choose Him instead of the world. Fearing God keeps us on mission. Fearing God establishes our position in Christ each and every single day that we are privileged to wake up and get out of bed.

If we choose to fear man and how we are perceived in this world, then we will always, ALWAYS fall short of what could be with God. But as we choose to fear God by seeking Him first and by letting His love cover us, our improper and unhealthy fear of man will become less of a hindrance in our faith journey. Don't you want that? I do, SO much! Will you pray this with me?

God, I've allowed the eyes and opinions of the world to exceed You in priority and in importance in my life. I'm so sorry for looking to them first and for questioning what You've placed in front of me. I choose to fear You today. I choose not just to respect You as Creator, but also to submit to You as the Sovereign, Just, and Righteous Lord of my life. Do what You need to do in my life. I love You. Amen.

22

GROWTH

. . . .

"Don't get so carried away with growing your business that you don't actually grow your relationship with God."

Jessica Hottle

I [Jessica] opened my journal and wrote these words, "The enemy likes to try and convince me that I'm not making an impact." "Where's my growth?" he says.

Growth. Is it always measurable?

As *she works His way* women, we work hard because we know we have a Father in Heaven who hears our prayers and we are ready to do our part. Women on mission. Women on mission to spread the gospel.

We don't work more (or harder) to prove ourselves to anyone.
We don't chase acknowledgments, fans, or likes.
We don't rush when patience runs dry.
We view others as friends, lead with love, and treat everyone as though they are an image-bearer of the Creator.

But, spreading the gospel message is not always measurable. Yes, we get to witness others being saved and sharing Jesus as their Lord, but we don't get to see all the women we inspire behind the screens of our phones or our computers.

In Matthew 10:1-16, Jesus sends out His twelve disciples with specific instructions for their missionary journey. He didn't just send them out; He also **"imparted to them authority to cast out demons and to heal every sickness and every disease." (v. 1)**

Just before their missionary journey, Jesus in Matthew chapter 9, talks about the **"The harvest truly is plentiful, but the laborers are few. Therefore pray the Lord of the harvest to send out laborers into His harvest." (vv. 37-38)**

He said this because He saw huge crowds of people and **"His heart was deeply**

47

moved with compassion because the people seemed weary and helpless, like wandering sheep without a Shepherd." (v. 36)

See, the enemy likes to try and convince me that my impact doesn't matter. Maybe you can relate? I can feel like showing up as I am is insignificant. I would like to believe that growth can simply mean being the one who goes out into the world, deeply moved with compassion, to help others discover that it's the Savior they are looking for.

I've often found that the things that are measurable when it comes to growth (like followers, likes, and subscribers) can easily distract us from the real growth He is calling us to rise to.

Friend, don't get so carried away with growing your business that you don't actually grow your relationship with God.

Remember, in the end, God always supplies the supernatural growth.

Father, if growing my business comes before growing my relationship with You, please show me. Nothing is more important to me than You and being Your daughter. I would be nothing without You. I love You! In Your name, Amen!

23

TOO FEW

· ·

"Rather than desiring more work for ourselves,
we need to pray for more to join us on mission."

Michelle Myers

It's typical to hear both business advice and Christian wisdom that goes like this:

Stay in your lane.

-or-

Keep focused on the work God has given you to do.

-or-

Don't consume yourself with what someone else is doing.

And while all of those statements certainly have their moments when they're true, I [Michelle] am afraid we are internalizing them so much that they're becoming more the norm, even among believers, than partnering together to do God's work.

Why don't we put this in *she works His way* terms we understand?

Solopreneurship is fine in business, but there's no place for solopreneurship in Kingdom work.

Let's go to God's Word together:

"But the priests were too few, so that they were unable to skin all the burnt offerings; therefore their brothers the Levites helped them until the work was completed and until the other priests had consecrated themselves. For the Levites were more conscientious to consecrate themselves than the priests." 2 Chronicles 29:34

After reading this in my devotion recently, I turned to similar words of Jesus:

"The harvest is plentiful, but the workers are few. Ask the Lord of the harvest, therefore, to send out workers into His harvest field." Luke 10:2

Both of these verses drive us to the same meaning:

1) In God's Kingdom, there's a lot of work to be done, and not a lot of us to do it.

Let's be honest: It's more common to be a casual Christian than a committed Christ-follower. *(And that's another devo for another day!)* In comparison with how many people are on this planet, there genuinely are few of us who are living for God's purposes. We must realize the realness of our assignment, along with its magnitude.

2) We must work together.

Because of the size and importance of our mission, we cannot isolate ourselves. Just like the Levites jumped in to help the priests, we need to look for ways to join God at work, even if it's not our "responsibility." Or even if someone else gets the "credit."

Pay attention where you see God at work and join Him there, even if it's as simple as being an encourager to those doing the heavy lifting.

3) Rather than desiring more work for ourselves, we need to pray for more to join us on mission.

Real question: Do you spend more time praying for God to send people you can help or will help you, or do your prayers reflect asking God to send more who will help in His mission?

There's no place for a scarcity mindset in Kingdom purposes. We serve an abundant God who can use each of us. Our prayers should reflect that.

Who can you encourage?
Who can you help?
Who can you partner with?
When will you pray for God to send more workers instead of sending more work for yourself?

Let's think bigger today, *she works His way.* Because our *real* mission is as big as the God we serve, and we can't do that alone.

God, thank You for my brothers and sisters who are living on mission. God, I pray You would send people into my path whom I can encourage. I pray that You would convict me often to jump in whenever possible to join others in Your work. Expand my mind to see past my personal ministry. God, right now, I ask that You would put in the hearts and minds of Your people to join us in Your work. We need more workers, Lord. Do only what You can do to reveal Yourself to those who don't know You. Help me to treat my co-workers in Christ like the gift they are. Rid my mind of the scarcity mentality, and help me to truly see the magnitude of Your work. It's not about me, God. It's about You. Help my actions truly reflect that. I love You. Amen.

24

PUSH THROUGH TO JESUS

. . . .

"Jesus doesn't just want us to look at Him through the crowd.
He wants us to push through and touch Him to receive healing."

Liz Patton

This morning over coffee, my husband asked me which moment in the Bible I [Liz] would most want to personally witness. Have you ever thought about that? I mean there are SO many amazing moments, right?

After thinking about it for probably too long, I finally decided on the woman who was bleeding for 12 years, whose faith healed her when she reached for Jesus. You can find this familiar story in Mark 5:21-34 and Luke 8:40-48.

What I find so interesting about this story is that it's kind of just mushed into the middle of what appears to be a more important story. Jesus was actually on His way to help the daughter of a synagogue ruler who was dying. As a synagogue ruler, this man must have had a prominent position in this culture.

But Jesus doesn't care about prominence. He sees us all the same – even this woman who had been bleeding for 12 years, who would have been considered defiled and unclean in her culture.

But she didn't let that stop her.

"She had suffered a great deal under the care of many doctors and had spent all she had, yet instead of getting better she grew worse. When she heard about Jesus, she came up behind him in the crowd and touched his cloak, because she thought, 'If I just touch his clothes, I will be healed.' Immediately her bleeding stopped and she felt in her body that she was freed from her suffering." **Mark 5:26-29**

What tremendous faith she must have had to believe that just touching Jesus would heal her. And unlike me, she didn't worry about what others thought of her!

She got up and pushed her way to Jesus. She didn't want to speak to Him or beg Him to heal her; nope, she simply wanted to touch the hem of his cloak to receive healing.

This inspires me so much and yet convicts me at the same time. Oh, that my faith would be this strong! Oh, that I wouldn't worry about how others perceive me! Just that I'd push my way through to Jesus.

I love how God's Word says that "immediately" she was healed and **"at once Jesus realized that power had gone from him."** (Mark 5:30). Boom. Just like that. Power spent. She was healed.

Jesus, being fully God, must have known who touched him, yet He asks "Who touched my clothes?" I think He wanted to give this woman, who had previously been shunned by her community, an opportunity to be publicly praised for her unwavering faith. In fact, He even calls her "Daughter." What love He has for His children!

Not only does Jesus refer to this woman *(who is never even given a name in Scripture)* as "Daughter," but don't you just love how He makes Himself available to be touched by her?! He doesn't just want us to look at Him through the crowd. He wants us to push through and touch Him!

I believe He is waiting for us to reach through the crowd, to stop worrying about what is socially acceptable, and push through to Him for healing. I doubt you need healing from 12 years of bleeding, but maybe it's a marriage that's been rocky, a prodigal child, a floundering business, or a disease or illness. Whatever it is, and however long you've been struggling, PUSH through to Jesus!

He doesn't just want you to look to Him; He wants you to reach out and touch Him. And when you do, picture Him saying, "**Daughter, your faith has healed you. Go in peace and be freed from your suffering.**" Mark 5:34

Dear God, thank You that You see us all the same. Thank You for making Yourself available to us. Strengthen our faith and our desire to reach out to You. Help us not worry what others think of us. Keep our eyes fixed only on You, our Great Physician. We love You. Amen.

25

LIFE-GIVER

. . . .

"Every person that we come in contact with on a daily basis
is a soul that may need Jesus."

Somer Phoebus

**"The words of a person's mouth are deep waters;
the fountain of wisdom is a bubbling brook."
Proverbs 18:4**

As women in the workplace who probably deal with people often, and who also
may be one of the only Christian influences in our work circle, the words that
come out of our mouths carry a lot of weight. I [Somer] can't help but wonder if
we truly comprehend that.

The verse above explains that our words can be life-giving water! They can be as
refreshing as a bubbling brook.

But they can also suck the life out of people.

I want to be a life-giver. I want to be "refreshing" in my conversations.

So often, we find ourselves moving from conversation to conversation throughout
the day, only giving thought to the subject matter and never to the person that
we're talking to. We are hyper-focused on the task that needs to be completed
but ignore the very thing that God has called us to do: Love His people.

As believers, most of us know that our calling is our ministry. We talk about that
often in the *she works His way* community. But do we understand that our calling,
whatever it is, will always be more about the people and less about the actual
work? Every person that we come in contact with on a daily basis is a soul that
may need Jesus.

Many of us have worked long and hard to get to where we are, so it makes
sense that our focus be the day-to-day grind of our career. That's not what God

intended though. You're where you are because He wants to use you for His glory, to reach His people, and to love them right into His arms.

How will you do that? By having conversations that give life and offer refreshment. Think about most of your work conversations - would you say that they are anything like that?

Lift up your head, take a look around, and see the people God has placed in front of you. See them for who they are and not what they can do for you. See them as lost souls that need to be pointed to the gospel and then, with your words, point them there!

God, give me a heart like Yours for those around me and help me not to be distracted with my tasks. Open their ears to Your truth and give me the words to share. Help me to SEE my customers and colleagues for who they are to You so that I can love them like You do. I love You. Amen.

26

DELIGHT IN THE SABBATH

. . . .

"Delighting in God isn't merely a matter of being un-distracted;
we must be uninterested in all other options."

Michelle Myers

"Mom, I am not a good rester!" Cole, my [Michelle] 4-year-old, declared after his first day of pre-K this year.

Before I could reply, my seven-year old, Noah, piped up from the back: "Mommy isn't either!"

I wanted to defend myself...but I knew he was right. And wow, sometimes, the brutal honesty of your kids is just the kick in the pants you need to stop simply *knowing* something is a struggle for you...and actually do something about it.

As God's Word is always on time, these words were part of my Bible reading just a few mornings later:

"If because of the Sabbath, you turn your foot
From doing your own pleasure on My holy day,
*And **call the Sabbath a delight,** the holy day of the Lord **honorable,***
And honor it, desisting from your own ways,
From seeking your own pleasure,
From speaking your own word,
Then you will take delight in the Lord,
And I will make you ride on the heights of the earth;
And I will feed you with the heritage of Jacob your father,
For the mouth of the Lord has spoken."
Isaiah 58:13-14

Instantly, I knew my problem.

It wasn't surface level. I do pretty well going through the motions of resting on Sundays. We serve at church, and then we come home so our youngest can nap.

56

My office door stays closed. I don't do much on social media, if anything at all. A lot of times, I'll even put my phone on the charger.

But do I delight in that? I'm embarrassed to say that up until a few weeks ago, more often than not, delight was not part of the process.

It wasn't that I didn't enjoy gathering with other believers at church or treasure the extra family time. I absolutely did. But I do believe there's a difference between enjoyment and delight.

Enjoyment means I am merely receiving pleasure or satisfaction. But *delighting* in something requires that I initiate my affections. Rather than just being an audience member, I become an engaged participant.

Let's give one more analogy. In addition to not being a good rester *(thanks, Cole!)*, I'm also the queen of having too many tabs open on my tech devices. So much so that eventually, my iMac surrenders and I can't get past the spinning rainbow of death without a reboot. Or my iPhone apps run so slowly that I waste an enormous amount of time just waiting for things to load.

she works His way, Sundays aren't for simply having everything else mindlessly running in the background. They're for being as plugged into Him as we are to our own lives every other day of the week.

Delighting in God isn't a matter of merely being un-distracted; we must be uninterested in all other options.

Let me say this same idea in a few different ways:

- The most productive way to begin your week is delighting in who God is and what He has done.

- If we don't genuinely delight in simply being in God's presence, we're longing for more of this world, not more of Heaven.

- Going through the motions of rest cannot fully recharge your spirit; only Jesus can.

If you feel like you go through the motions of "resting" on a Sabbath, but come Monday, you simply feel like all you did was waste a day of potential productivity, let me offer you a challenge:

Live out the difference between enjoyment and delight. See if that doesn't open up levels of contentment and satisfaction you've never experienced before.

Pray this with me (and let's pray this often!):

God, it is the greatest joy of my life to know You and to live for You. Today is Your day, not mine. Rid my mind of the things of this world so I can fully delight in who You are and what You've done. Fill me because I know You are the only One who can. I love You. Amen.

27

SLAVERY TO FREEDOM

. . . .

"More effort doesn't equal more money
or a promised rank advancement."

Jessica Hottle

God sent His son to set us free. It's our job to stay free and help others be set free.

Let's take an inventory, how free are you really feeling today?

Are you. . .

Thinking about how you don't think you are meant for business?
Thinking about how you think you fail as a leader?
Thinking about how you feel you should be further along?
Thinking about how there's so much to do and you don't even know where to start?

If what you are thinking isn't producing fruit, then it's not His thoughts about you.

Let's take another inventory, how often are you working *for* freedom and not *from* it?

"I [Jessica] am just going to work a little longer today so I can rest later," I would say to myself.

Hours pass.

Still working.

"Okay, I've just got to finish this up and then I'll be done for the day," I would continue to say. "Oh wait, I can do that really quick first," is another phrase I would often say.

I would convince myself that I was being productive and "working," but really, I was working for my freedom. I was working because, if I didn't work, who else was going to do it? I was afraid of not producing results because I thought more effort = more money, rank advancement, you name it.

Let me be so bold to call it what it was: slavery. I was a slave to my work.

There wasn't freedom when I was chained to my results, opinions of others, and the thoughts of whether I would be successful or not.

I was a slave to it.

God kept inviting me in to rest. "Are you going to allow any room for me to work, Jess?" I felt He would say to me at times.

That's when I would jump on social media and start scrolling. The longer I scrolled, the longer I began to believe I wasn't good enough for the mission the Lord had given me.

Soon enough you'll start chasing someone else's dreams before asking yourself if God ever asked you to go there in the first place. Social media can be a tricky thing if you aren't intentional about how you navigate through the noise and through the blessings. The more you realize her life is hers and she isn't your competition or enemy, then the more you'll realize your life has its own blessings specifically for you.

It is our responsibility to live in our freedom no matter what we feel we should be doing or where we think we should be in our life.

Paul writes in Ephesians 6:20, *"I may preach the wonderful news of God's kingdom with bold freedom at every opportunity. Even though I am chained as a prisoner, I am His ambassador."*

What we feel or think isn't always who we are. What we get to do is because of what Jesus did on the cross. It's an opportunity - not a prison sentence.

You are no longer a slave, friend. You are free indeed.

Stop scrolling and start asking God to show you His mission and blessings for you.

Father, help us to keep working from a place of freedom and not for it. Remove anything in our lives that keeps taking us away from the main thing: You. No amount of work determines our worth. We are so in love with You! Amen!

28

UNSEEN

. . . .

"Your influence for the kingdom is not based on how much you do that is seen by others, but rather by how much you obey God based on the things that you believe, but can't see."

Emily Copeland

Our actions are the clearest indications of what we believe, right? A simple example of this would be that my girls believed that they would be getting Christmas presents based on their behavior, so they were little angels on Christmas morning. They obeyed their mom and dad because they believed good behavior would yield a reward (and I [Emily] am still picking up little LOL Doll clothing out of the carpet.)

How often do we act on something that we believe versus something that we know?

"For our light and momentary troubles are achieving for us an eternal glory that far outweighs them all. So we fix our eyes not on what is seen, but on what is unseen, since what is seen is temporary, but what is unseen is eternal." 2 Corinthians 4:17-18

Think about your work. Whether you work in the corporate world or you are home raising children, your influence for the kingdom is not based on how much you do that is seen by others, but rather by how much you obey God based on the things that you believe, but can't see.

You have influence. I have influence. Every person has influence, but if our influence doesn't lead people to obey what God has commanded us even when we can't see the outcome, then it's wasted and we can't call it faith.

Is God really faithful? If you believe the answer is yes, then people will be influenced towards Jesus by the way that you live your life giving it all back to Him.

"If we are faithless, He remains faithful, for He cannot deny Himself." 2 Timothy 2:13

Are God's promises reliable? If you answer 'yes' then you will give people hope by the way you rely on Him when hard seasons come.

"And this same God who takes care of me will supply all your needs from his glorious riches, which have been given to us in Christ Jesus." Philippians 4:19

Will God really get the glory? When we believe that God will get the glory the way that He says He will, then we will live our lives in a way that has other people's best interest in mind and we won't work hard to earn it for ourselves.

"All this is for your benefit, so that the grace that is reaching more and more people may cause thanksgiving to overflow to the glory of God." 2 Corinthians 4:15

Does my integrity in my work really make an impact? God's Word says "Yes!" Doing the right thing is not always noticed. But when it is, it is powerful to the people around you. Don't ever underestimate integrity and the influence that it gives you for the kingdom.

"The integrity of the upright guides them, but the unfaithful are destroyed by their duplicity." Proverbs 11:3

The world lives by its own version of truth. What they need is for our lives to be a pillar of hope because of the way we live by faith. We get to show them what it's like to obey God's Word and watch Him change our hearts and lives in the process. Step out in faith today. Do what God asks of you, even if it won't make sense to anyone around you. Trust God with the results. He is the greatest thing that we cannot see.

God, thank You for fulfilling Your promises so that faith becomes one of our greatest privileges. Help us to choose You boldly today even when it cannot be explained. We're holding onto every word You say today. We love You! Amen.

29

CLEAN UP

. . . .

"We're handcuffing ourselves to sin instead of
making ourselves at home in Christ."

Somer Phoebus

If left alone growing up, my brother, sister, and I [Somer] would have a grand
time destroying our house. Dishes everywhere, towels on the bathroom floor, and
every food item out of the fridge and cupboards to be left on the counters half-
eaten. I'm not gonna lie - we loved having the house to ourselves.

But then we'd get the call...the "we're on our way home" call. And we'd jump
into action. We couldn't welcome our parents home with the house in disarray.
Not unless we wanted to deal with a punishment.

The clean-up was always miserable, and even at a young age I remember thinking,
Why did we let it get like this? We know better!

The freedom wasn't worth the work it took to get it back in order.

In Romans 13:11-14 Paul gives God's holy people of Rome a reminder...

**"Besides this you know the time, that the hour has come for you to wake
from sleep. For salvation is nearer to us now than when we first believed.
The night is far gone; the day is at hand. So then let us cast off the works
of darkness and put on the armor of light. Let us walk properly as in the
daytime, not in orgies and drunkenness, not in sexual immorality and
sensuality, not in quarreling and jealousy. But put on the Lord Jesus Christ,
and make no provision for the flesh, to gratify its desires."**

Paul loved these people, but he knew some of them were gambling with their
lives. They were living according to their own desires and not to the ways of God.
He reminded them that God is real and He is coming back for His people. You
have to remember back in those days there were so many false gods that were
made of stone or gold that offered people nothing but rules and rituals to follow

and no hope for their future. It was easy to get sidetracked and forget for a second that our God was a living, breathing, all-knowing, omnipresent God, that He had a plan and that His plan would include coming back for us. Paul reminded the people of who God really was.

He charged them to get serious about their faith. He told them to cast off the darkness and put on the light, to quit living in sin and answering to their flesh!

Just like my siblings and I thought we were experiencing freedom without our parents around, believers sometimes live their lives the same way – giving in to our wants instead of surrendering to God's plans. But, at some point, we all realize that's not freedom at all. That's the worst kind of bondage. We're basically handcuffing ourselves to sin instead of making ourselves at home in Christ.

In our story growing up, there was a phone call to warn that mom and dad were on their way. There's not a phone call when it comes to the return of Jesus. And even if there was, do you really want to live in such a way that you would have to get things in order before He came for you?

How messy is your spiritual life?

How cluttered is your heart?

Are you living for you or are you living for Him?

Paul didn't want bondage for the people of Rome *(or those of us reading his words today)* so let this passage motivate you to get your life in order! Let's be ready to meet Jesus with our lives in order and our hands busy in HIS work.

God, show me the areas of my life I need to clean up. Forgive me for blurring the lines of what I want and what You've told me I need. I ask that You will help me to feel the urgency to live my life for You so that I can anticipate Your return rather than fear it. God, thank You for Your Word that shows me how to be a better follower of You. I love You. Amen.

30

BE HERE NOW

. . . .

"No matter what season you're in with your family or
what stage you're in with your business—embrace this place!
Where you are right now is God's place for you!"

Liz Patton

I [Liz] can vividly remember being in the nursery with my boys at church when
they were little babies, with boogers on my dress and cold coffee in my hand.
One of the older women in our congregation came up to me and lovingly said,
"Oh honey, just enjoy this time! They'll be grown before you know it!" I honestly
just wanted a good night's sleep, a clean dress, and a hot cup of coffee.

As I look back at that season of my life, it's so obvious to me that, even though
some of those days of my boys being little may have seemed long, the years have
been so very short! I'm so grateful that I learned to embrace the crazy instead of
wishing it away.

But if I'm really honest with myself, I still have a tendency to look forward to
what's next more than be fully present where I am right now. Maybe you can
relate. For example, do you ever say to yourself:

- When I finally get to the next level in my business, then I'll be able to "fill
  in the blank."

- When I finally have my website just right, I'll share it with others.

- When I finally have my newsletter perfect, then I'll send it.

- When I finally get to Friday, then I can relax.

- When I finally feel comfortable in my own skin, then I'll be happy.

- When I finally grow my business a little larger, then I can create better
  boundaries and more margins.

Life is short, friends! We need to Be. Here. Now!

In 1 Corinthians 7:17 of the Message translation, Paul says,

*"And don't be wishing you were someplace else or with someone else. Where you are right now is God's place for you. **Live** and **obey** and **love** and **believe right there.**"* I couldn't possibly love this anymore!

I want to encourage you today, no matter what season you're in with your family or what stage you're in with your business—embrace this place! Where you are right now is God's place for you!

If we break down Paul's instruction to us, there are four simple things we can do today to be here now:

Live. We aren't truly living if we are constantly waiting for what's right up ahead. Planning for the future is fine, but make a concerted effort to be grateful for the season you're in. We don't get this day back again.

Obey. Here at *she works His way*, we define success as obedience. You don't have to do it like the rest of the world is doing it. Keep your eyes fixed on Jesus and walk in obedience to what He's calling you to do.

Love. If we remember that our main purpose as believers is to love God and to love others, it helps us be fully present in the moment. We don't need to complicate it. Just love.

Believe right there. Believe you have what it takes for the job right where you are. Believe you are where you're supposed to be. In this moment. Right now and right here. And believe fully in the God who has called you to this season.

Dear God, I want to be here now. I want to be fully present and embrace this season I'm in. Help me to stop looking ahead for what's to come and instead fully savor where I am today. I trust that You are in control of my past, present, and future, and I put my life in Your all-sufficient hands. I love You, and I trust You. Amen.

31

CHARACTER > CHARISMA

. . . .

"Charisma becomes a problem when it exists
in the absence of Christ-like character."

Michelle Myers

James and I [Michelle] just binge-watched *Waco*, the mini-series on the Paramount Network about David Koresh and the Branch Davidians. Every episode, I watched in horror as they told the true story of the two-month standoff between Koresh and the FBI that ultimately resulted in the loss of over 80 lives.

Included in that 80 were not just radical followers of Koresh – but innocent children.

Koresh's views were radical. But even more than that, the way Koresh lived greatly contradicted the Bible he claimed to preach.

So how were so many people fooled by him, even to the point of losing their own lives and the lives of their children?

Charisma.

You know the type. When they walk into a room, they turn heads. When they talk, people listen. They know how to say what people want to hear. And it's not just about the words they say, but how they make people feel in the way they say them.

Now, not all charisma is bad. But charisma becomes a problem when it exists in the absence of Christ-like character.

We see the same problem in 2 Samuel when we look at the life of David's son, Absalom.

Absalom was a smooth-talker. Super personable. 2 Samuel 15:1-6 details how Absalom would intentionally get up early in the morning to stand in the city gates, schmooze people over who came to see the king, and eventually, steal their loyalty away from his father, King David.

Absalom typically said the right things, but his actions were more than questionable...

There was the time Absalom set Joab's field on fire *(2 Samuel 14:28-30)*.

Or the time he committed adultery with his father's concubines while all of Israel watched *(2 Samuel 16:22)*.

Yet, we learn that *"the people increased continually with Absalom"* *(2 Samuel 15:12)*. They chose Absalom's charisma over David's Christ-like character.

But charisma could only carry him so far. Absalom surrounded himself with ungodly and wicked advisors who ultimately led him to his own death *(2 Samuel 18:9-14)* through a plan God ordained to bring David back to power *(2 Samuel 17:14)*.

So what does this mean for us?

As leaders:
- We should rely on God's Word to guide and influence others more than our personality or talents.

- We should desire for others to be more in awe of God than they are of us.

- We should aim to win them to Christ, rather than aim to win people over to ourselves.

For leaders we choose to follow:
- Charisma can be present, but character should be more evident than personality.

- They must believe in ways that are consistent with what they claim to believe.

- Passion should not outweigh wisdom.

One final caution: It may be relatively simple to spot charismatic leaders with no depth in real life, but because we can be selective about what we share online, it's much easier to be digitally deceived.

This is why it's so important that we are grounded in God's Word. His Word is truth, and knowing truth makes it much easier to spot lies. As we seek His wisdom, we grow in discernment and in lasting knowledge.

But if we aren't grounding ourselves in what the Bible teaches, we won't know truth, friends, and we are much more likely to find ourselves following a false teacher. It's that simple.

*It doesn't matter how funny/inspiring/competent she is...*if she's feeding you falsehood.

*It doesn't matter how justified she makes you feel in your fleshly desires...*if she's elevating her own opinion over what God's Word says.

*It doesn't matter how others are following her...*if she's not following Christ.

*Just because she says the name of Jesus...*that doesn't mean she's living for Him.

The Bible warns us that the world is full of people we shouldn't follow...and because of social media, we have easy access to follow more and more of them.

The only real way we can ensure we aren't led astray is by intentionally following Jesus first and foremost, friends. Let's be leaders who prioritize Christ – not charisma.

God, thank You for the warnings in Scripture to show us the consequences of living for ourselves vs. living for You. God, help me treasure Your truth. Imprint Your words on my heart so that I can easily recognize those who are far from You. Give me a spirit of discernment to know who to follow and who to avoid. Mold me into a leader that others can follow, not because of who I am, but because I am following You. I love You. Amen.

32

HAPPY HERO

. . . .

"God didn't DIE for us just so that we could live for ourselves."

Somer Phoebus

I [Somer] am in the midst of reading Ezekiel with our *she works His way* community, and let me just make one thing clear: I'm 12 chapters in and there hasn't been one feel-good moment yet.

There's been fighting, death, head-shaving, transformer type creature-machines, and God's wrath, LOTS AND LOTS of God's wrath, but no joyful plot twist.

While I know the Bible to be 100% true in its ENTIRETY, unfortunately I am realizing as I get older that I have spent most of my life giving more attention and study time to the feel-good parts. The redeeming stories, the miracles, the lives that were saved and transformed by the power of the gospel. But to give my attention to only those sections of Scripture is to deny who God really is.

I've put Him in another box - we tend to do that as believers. If this box were labeled, it would be called my *Happy Hero* box. How ridiculous does that sound when we think about God though? He's so much more than a *Happy Hero*, but that's how we like to see Him.

Yes, He loves us. **(John 3:16)**
Yes, He's a friend that sticks closer than a brother. **(Proverbs 18:24)**
Yes, He cares about even the little things in our lives and carries our burdens. **(Psalm 55:22)**

But He's also jealous for us! And wouldn't that make sense? If He loves us so much, how could He not be jealous for us? **(Deuteronomy 4:23-24)**

The book of Ezekiel gives us an in-depth look at how those stinkin' Israelites just don't get it (like we often don't), so once again God had to show them who He really was and it wasn't pretty! It was actually pretty terrifying.

We were raised as children listening to the "good" Bible stories, the ones with the happy endings, so now it's only reasonable that we would think of God as He was portrayed by our 3rd grade Sunday School teacher - the *Happy Hero*.

As adults we leave those *Happy Hero* stories behind but only to move to the adult version: The Prosperous Hero. Those are all about a very generous God who pours out His blessings on His people and provides abundantly more than we ever could have hoped. **(Ephesians 3:20)**

Here's what we need to understand though: God is all of those things. He is the hero of our lives, and He does give us abundantly more when we're seeking Him first. But He's also a jealous God, He HATES sin and He HATES when we tolerate it.

You see, God can't be one without the other. He can't be loving and not care what we do. He can't provide for us and not care how we steward His provision. He can't fight for us only to let us run when we feel like it. And He didn't DIE for us so that we could live for ourselves.

Today, can we take a minute to understand who God really is? I think if we do that, it will change the way we live.

"In the fear of the LORD there is strong confidence, And his children will have refuge. The fear of the LORD is a fountain of life, That one may avoid the snares of death." Proverbs 14:26-27

Dear God, I'm so thankful that You are a loving God and I'm so sorry for when I forget that You are also a jealous God. Help me to see You for who You really are and not just who I want to see You as. I pray that You would convict me when I sin and make me miserable when I'm not walking with You. God, You are all mighty, all powerful, and I love You! Amen.

33

YOUR WORK, YOUR WAY

. . . .

"You are more than a number and
so is the mission you are called to."

Jessica Hottle

Likes on Facebook.
Followers on Twitter.
Views on Instagram Stories.
Subscribers on Youtube.

None of it matters if we detach ourselves from the main Source. If God isn't the Source, then all we are doing is racing to see who can be the busiest and have the most people who we don't even know follow and "like" us.

There is so much pressure to look the best, be the best, have the most followers (because then you are considered to be someone who knows what they are talking about), and make the most money.

But for what?

Please know that when I [Jessica] say this, I'm not saying that any of those things are bad. I don't believe it's ever the intention of *she works His way* women to say the tools or resources we have access to, like social media, are bad in any way.

The only question I pose here is: Does social media have you or do you have social media? Who is controlling whom?

More followers do not equal more money.
More views do not mean more significance.
More likes do not equal more intelligence.

The pressure is real though, my friend. I have allowed myself to feel this pressure. I have been told by others many times, "Jess, you should have done better than that when you look at the numbers." I'm sure they meant it to be constructive, but when attached with how good I am or not good I am, it becomes destructive.

Do numbers help us? Yes. For sure.
Can numbers guide us and give us direction? Yep. You bet.
Can numbers harm us, when attached with measuring how good you are or are not? Absolutely yes!

As soon as we give emotional weight to numbers, we have lost sight of why we do what we do.

Kris Vallotton said on his podcast, "There is so much pressure to be nowhere first." Often, I don't think we even know what we are chasing, let alone why we are chasing it.

Chasing numbers is like chasing after the wind. It will never be enough.

Ecclesiastes 2:11 says *"Yet when I surveyed all that my hands had done and what I had toiled to achieve, everything was meaningless, a chasing after the wind; nothing was gained under the sun."*

Chasing the heart of the Father is where you will find your way, not get lost, rest when everyone else is racing, and be calm when the pressure seems strong.

You are more than a number and so is the mission you are called to.

Let this be your prayer today: *Father, it's Your words, Your work. Your work, Your way. Your way, Your win. Amen!*

34

GRATITUDE MULTIPLIES THE BLESSING

. . . .

"When expressing gratitude before the blessing becomes a habit, whether the blessing happens or not becomes insignificant, because our hearts are filled with joy, peace, gratitude, and contentment!"

Liz Patton

Gratitude is a pretty big deal in our house. I [Liz] personally love keeping a daily gratitude list, and we encourage our boys to regularly remember what they have to be thankful for. I'm pretty sure that if you are reading this, you probably do the same. I've just found that it's so much easier to be content when we focus on what we DO have rather than focus on what we don't have.

Recently, I noticed that in God's Word, there are multiple examples of gratitude actually multiplying God's blessing! So often we think about expressing gratitude AFTER the blessing, but what if we changed this around and thanked God BEFORE?!

Take a look with me at the example of Jesus thanking His Father for hearing Him before He raises Lazarus from the dead in John 11:41-42:

"Then Jesus looked up and said, "Father, I <u>thank you</u> that you have heard me. I knew that you always hear me, but I said this for the benefit of the people standing here, that they may believe that you sent me. When he had said this, Jesus called in a loud voice, "Lazarus, come out!" The dead man came out, his hands and feet wrapped with strips of linen, and a cloth around his face. Jesus said to them, "Take off the grave clothes and let him go."

I'm sure that Jesus, Martha, Mary, AND Lazarus were all beyond grateful after Jesus raised Lazarus from the dead, but His expression for this gratitude was expressed before the miracle even happened. Not after.

Another example of Jesus expressing gratitude that multiplies the blessing is found in Matthew 15:36-37 when Jesus feeds the four thousand:

"Then he took the seven loaves and the fish, and <u>when he had given thanks</u>, he broke them and gave them to the disciples, and they in turn to the people. They all ate and were satisfied. Afterward the disciples picked up seven basket-fulls of broken pieces that were left over."

Again, I'm sure Jesus and the disciples were elated that there was enough food to feed everyone when they realized there was food left over. But the thanks was given when Jesus only had seven loaves and fish.

If we relate this to our lives today, can we do the same as Jesus—can we be grateful before we receive the blessing, when we don't even know if the blessing will be given? Can we thank God for a marriage that feels rocky *(or maybe hasn't even happened yet)*, a nursery that is still empty, a business that hasn't provided financially, a prodigal child that hasn't returned home, or whatever dream or goal that hasn't yet happened?

Let's just say it like it is—it's tough stuff. It's not easy to do. Just like I'm sure it wasn't easy for Jesus to thank His Father when one of His best friends laid dead in a tomb. And just like I'm sure it wasn't easy for Him to appear foolish in front of a group of thousands to thank God for seven measly loaves of bread and fish. But, Jesus wasn't focusing on His circumstances – He was focusing on His Father!

And we can do the same! When expressing gratitude before the blessing becomes a habit, whether the blessing happens or not becomes insignificant because our hearts are filled with joy, peace, gratitude, and contentment! And isn't that the biggest blessing of all?

Dear God, thank You! Thank You for loving me, seeing me, and hearing me. Thank You for all of the blessings You've given me in the past that I didn't even see because I was so focused on myself. Help me to always remember to express my gratitude to You FIRST. May thankfulness always be on my lips. I love You with my whole heart for my whole life. Amen.

35

PROTECTED

. . . .

"Your mission, your work, your vision- when given by God- will be fiercely protected by Him as well."

Emily Copeland

Protection. It's one of the highest needs of a woman. Not because we are weak, but because we are stronger at identifying needs and then meeting them for everyone around us. We all long for protection physically, and also emotionally, and spiritually. Listen, they haven't given defensive moms the name "momma bear" for nothing! We value protection fiercely, down to our core. And so does God.

"So do not fear, for I am with you; do not be dismayed, for I am your God. I will strengthen you and help you; I will uphold you with my righteous right hand." Isaiah 41:10

So let's talk about how God protects us in our work and in raising a family. Without question, you will never be better protected by anyone the way that you are by God. Your mission, your work, your vision – when given by God – will be protected fiercely by Him as well. But before we dig deeper there, we must remember that God's protection in your life is not based on merit or by your level of faith. God's protection is based on His unwavering LOVE for you. He can do much when your dream is placed in His hands. But, protection isn't just safety from unhealthy things or being shielded from harm. Protection also means removing things (even good things) from our lives and our paths that will keep us from Him.

Will He say "no" to things that seem good for us? Yes. Will He take away business opportunities or coworkers? Possibly. Will He protect us from dangerous things that we are blind to like money and fame? Yes. Will He allow us to fail so that we can see Him better from our view on the ground? I think we can all say YES. Is He still a Good God and a Perfect Father? More than we could even fathom!

"But the Lord is faithful, and He will strengthen you and protect you from the evil one." 2 Thessalonian 3:3

The blessing doesn't come from resting in a safe place...the blessing is found in knowing God's heart for you is gracious and giving. The blessing is in raised, empty, and surrendered hands – not in the more comfortable white-knuckled grips. Protection in our work and in our family is God's to choose and ours to trust.

God, thank You for being our Fierce Protector. As You move and work in our lives, help us to remember that every move You make is for our good. You are not on the lookout to punish, but rather to protect Your Spirit in us and our mission at hand. You're a Good God. We love You! Amen.

36

HIGHLIGHT REEL

. . . .

"Your online presence should be the overflow of your life offline."

Jessica Hottle

Paul's Highlight Reel

"As Paul gathered an armful of sticks and was laying them on the fire, a poisonous snake, driven out by the heat, bit him on the hand. The people of the island saw it hanging from his hand and said to each other, "A murderer, no doubt! Though he escaped the sea, justice will not permit him to live." But Paul shook off the snake into the fire and was unharmed." Acts 28:3-5

"Then some Jews came from Antioch and Iconium and won the crowd over. They stoned Paul and dragged him outside the city, thinking he was dead. But after the disciples had gathered around him, he got up and went back into the city." Acts 14:19-20

"She [woman who had a spirit that predicted the future] followed Paul and the rest of us, shouting, "These men are servants of the Most High God, who are telling you the way to be saved." She kept this up for many days. Finally, Paul became so annoyed that he turned around and said to the spirit, "In the name of Jesus Christ I command you to come out of her!" At that moment, the spirit left her. When her owners realized that their hope of making money was gone, they seized Paul and Silas and dragged them into the marketplace to face the authorities." Acts 16:17-19

Our Highlight Reel:

Pretty photos on social media where everything is put together, in place, and gives the illusion that you struggle with nothing, have it all together (*because, hey, with God all things are possible*), and have a deep and intimate relationship with the Father.

I [Jessica] think the list could go on in describing what we deem as worthy of a highlight reel. Am I right?

It's easy to post really cute Bible verses but never live like the verse that you just quoted. It's way easier to show you have it all together than to simply be vulnerable and humble enough to know you don't and you need help.

How much of Paul's life was spent in prison, jail, and in chains, yet his attitude remained the same?

In the Bible we read the miracles, signs, and wonders, but we also read about the things many people experienced for speaking truth and bringing light. The outcome for living boldly for Christ didn't always bring more followers, more money, or more fame.

But, my friend, this isn't bad news. It's only bad news if those were the things we were chasing in the first place.

We relate to people on a deeper level because we find ourselves in their stories.

Think about it.

If God only chose to use people and stories that talked about them laying around on beach chairs and soaking up the sun while listening to the gospel, it would be really hard to relate to them, because that's not what "real" life looks like day in and day out.

I'm all for the pretty photos. But let's be careful to not cause our sister to stumble either by only showing the "perfect" versions of ourselves. As leaders, as *she works His way* women, we have a responsibility to lead well and with truth – the whole truth.

You have influence, whether it is face-to-face with one person or on social media with 500 followers.

"But take care that this right of yours does not somehow become a stumbling block to the weak." 1 Corinthians 8:9

Although Paul was talking about food offered to idols in this passage, I think it's the same for us today in social media.

Let's not lead double lives, sisters. As our founder, Michelle Myers, once said, "Let's live better offline, then online."

Your online presence should be the overflow of your offline life. You don't have to have it all together and be perfect for someone to be changed by the gospel. (We see that with Paul's story.)

Changing people is God's job. It's our job to show up out of obedience so He can take care of the rest.

Father, thank You for Your grace. Thank You for new opportunities every day. Help me to become more like You with every chance that I get. Let my highlight reel look more and more like real life in the trenches with You than some made up gospel to get more of something I want. We love You, Father! Amen!

37

CLING TO HIM!

. . . .

"It's not the visibility of the path that matters,
it's the faith you have in your Guide."

Somer Phoebus

My [Somer] daughter is an extreme over-thinker which results in her being very indecisive. She is so terrible at making decisions that we often get frustrated at her inability to make a call on simple things, like what she wants to eat. My daughter, Kennedi, is the kind of person who prefers clear direction. Like crystal CLEAR.

As believers, our mission is clear but the exact steps to get there may be a little less clear. Is God trying to confuse us or make it difficult for us to follow Him? No! He just wants our undivided attention, and undivided attention comes when there's nothing else to look at but Him.

Have you ever been blindfolded? Maybe walking into a surprise party or for some kind of game? In those moments when you couldn't see, did you cling a little closer to the person guiding you? Of course you did.

As we take steps into our future, we have to be okay with a blurry view. We have to be okay with unanswered questions, confusing situations, and uncertain timelines. At those moments, we should cling a little closer to our Jesus. That's when we start to understand what it looks like to actually have FAITH.

Our church walked through a series on Abraham right, and let me tell you, I want the faith that Abraham had.

In Genesis 22, God asked Abraham to sacrifice his only son, Isaac. In an incredible, giant, enormous leap of faith, Abraham tells God "yes." God then stops Abraham from killing his son and we see one of the most intense tests of the Bible.

Abraham didn't have answers; what God asked him to do didn't make sense nor was it easy, but in that moment Abraham clung to God and knew that His ways were better! His thoughts were higher, and obedience was the only option.

When you can't see the details of His plan, is obedience your only option?

We talk in business all the time about non-negotiables, but we usually refer to them when we're talking about those things that WE'VE decided are non-negotiable. But God has non-negotiables for us too! Obedience is one of them.

You've heard it said that partial obedience is disobedience. So if partial obedience is disobedience, wouldn't that mean that partial faith isn't really faith at all? You can't keep calling out to your "sovereign God" and then forget He is sovereign when the story doesn't play out the way you wanted it to. He is either all good, or He's not! He is either in control or He's not!

It's time to be okay with an unclear, bumpy, and somewhat hidden path because the visibility of the path doesn't matter. The Guide however, does! Do you have complete and total faith in your guide?

Cling to Him! He will make your paths straight! **(Proverbs 3:5-6)**

God, show Yourself to me! Help me to focus on what You're doing in my life and not on the circumstances of my days. I want to be like Abraham. Give me faith to obey You. Thank You for loving me! Amen.

38

MAKE A JOYFUL NOISE

. . . .

"We all have gifts that can be used to worship the Giver of our gifts.
Even if it sounds like it's noise to you, I promise that your
Creator hears it as the sweetest song."

Liz Patton

Last night our small-town church in rural Virginia hosted the Contemporary Christian praise band, Citizen Way, for a concert for our local community. As you can imagine, the concert was absolutely amazing, and the worship experience was more than I [Liz] could have hoped for. But the conversation around my kitchen counter when we got home from the concert taught me a lesson I think I'll remember forever.

The car ride home was loud and full of excitement, so after we got home and things quieted down a little bit, my 11-year-old-son said to me, "Mama, that band sounded exactly like Citizen Way." *(I swear I couldn't make this up if I tried, y'all.)*

And I said, "You know why they sounded exactly like Citizen Way? Because they WERE Citizen Way!!"

We both laughed until I cried. He said he wondered why we were making such a big deal out of a group just singing someone else's songs. I guess in his mind there was no way the REAL band would come to our little town.

This morning during my quiet time, I felt God stir in my heart that it didn't make any difference to Him at all whether it was Citizen Way worshiping Him or simply just our small town church. He just loved that we were doing what Psalm 98:4 tells us to do:

"Make a joyful noise to the Lord, all the earth;
break forth into joyous song and sing praises!"

When I looked at my son during that concert last night, he was ALL IN! He was praising His Savior and it didn't matter to him one little bit if it was the real-deal Citizen Way or not.

Sister, let me ask you—are you ALL IN using the gifts that God has given you, or are you holding back because you don't think you are the real deal? Are you making a joyful noise to the Lord in your worship, with your family, and in your business? Or are you shrinking back because you don't think you are equipped enough?

I want to encourage you today to worship as loud as you can! Not only is God praised when we worship, but we are changed! And when I say "worship," I'm not just talking about singing. You can worship God with your workout, with your social media posts *(no matter how big or small your "platform" is)*, with a conversation you have with your high-schooler, with a handwritten note to encourage a friend, or with a dinner you deliver to a sick neighbor.

We all have gifts that can be used to worship the Giver of our gifts. Even if it sounds like it's noise to you, I promise that your Creator hears it as the sweetest song.

"He put a new song in my mouth,
   a hymn of praise to our God.
Many will see and fear the Lord
   and put their trust in him."
Psalm 40:3

Dear God, today I worship You! Thank You for the gifts You have given me. Forgive me for the times I have taken these gifts for granted. Show me unique and creative ways to use my gifts so that You are glorified and so that others see You in me and want to know more about You. I lift Your name on high! I love You with my whole heart. Amen.

39

ATTRACTIVE LIARS

. . . .

"Lies often sound better than the truth,
and liars can draw large crowds."

Michelle Myers

A few years ago, I [Michelle] started making personalized notes in my Bible for my oldest son, Noah, as this will be the Bible I pass down to him. Usually, a lot of things I write here are similar to the notes I leave for him in the margins.

Occasionally, though, I get super blunt with him…and usually, it has to do with false teachers. Because false prophets are not a thing of the past. In fact, thanks to the device in your hand, we now have access to more of them than ever before.

So in the margins of Ezekiel 13, here's what I wrote to Noah:

Lies often sound better than the truth, and liars can draw large crowds.

Here's how Ezekiel put it:

*"Son of man, prophesy against the prophets of Israel who **prophesy and say to those who prophesy from their own inspiration,** 'Listen to the word of the Lord!' Thus says the Lord God, 'Woe to the foolish prophets **who are following their own spirit and have seen nothing.'"** Ezekiel 13:2-3*

Prophesying from their own inspiration. Following their own spirit.

Later, in Ezekiel 13:6, he not only calls their words a false vision, but goes as far as to say their teachings were lying divination. *(See? Ezekiel started the liar talk!)*

Basically, what was happening is that Ezekiel was genuinely hearing a prophetic warning from the Lord, begging the Israelites to repent of their sin and turn back to God. Meanwhile, the false prophets were giving a completely different message: condoning the people's sinful lifestyles and telling them everything was fine.

The people chose to listen to the message that was easier to hear.

Sweet friends, let's not make the same mistake.

The only way to identify a false teacher from a genuine teacher is by listening to the message and measuring what they say with what God's Word says.

False teachers change God's message to align with their own agenda.

Genuine teachers stick to the truths God's Word says.

Even when they can't fully understand it or explain it.
Even when it doesn't "feel good."
Even when it's super unpopular.

So in a world where it's becoming increasingly different to know authentic from fake faith, how do we protect ourselves?

Read the Bible for yourself daily.

You can't spot lies (or even more difficult to identify– *twisted* truth!) when you don't know what God's Word says. This is our foundation as believers, and there are no substitutes.

Pray for discernment.

Don't rely on simply a quick judge of character. Ask God to help you discern His voice from other voices.

Don't cheapen faith to merely on-line involvement.

We may be an online community for Christian women, but I'll say it again: *she works HIS way* is in no shape, form, or fashion a replacement for being involved in a local church. Strengthen your personal walk with the Lord by doing life alongside, worshipping, and serving God among other believers in your city.

Beware whenever you are encouraged to self-sufficiency.

John 15:5 is clear that, apart from God, we can do nothing. So in a world where the #girlBOSS and #thefutureisfemale messages are prevalent, understand that anything that points us to pull from within ourselves rather than reach up to God, is at best a message to listen to with caution.

God's message should always leave us in awe of God, not ourselves.

As a culture, we're becoming increasingly narcissistic. And while we can always learn something for ourselves as we read the Bible, we can't miss that the book is about God and His story. Beware of teachers who tell you more about how to live your life than the One who gave you life.

We must be on our guard, *she works His way*. The devil has many schemes to deceive us, and false teachers are part of his plan. Let's refuse to be misled by them.

God, thank You for Your Word. Help us to be faithful in reading it and doing what it says. God, fill us with Your discernment to know Your voice among the many voices that compete for our attention each day. Be loud in our lives, Lord. We want to follow You and listen only to those who are following You. We love You. Amen.

40

EXCEL SHEET FAITH

. . . .

*"Our greatest concern with the call from God
should never be the 'how', only the 'who.'"*

Emily Copeland

Have you ever felt the Holy Spirit nudging you to say something or do something in an unexpected moment? I [Emily] tend to get this most at the cash register when I'm checking out at the grocery store. My first thought is, "Really? Right here? Now?", then I review my plan to exit as quickly as possible so that my kids don't break anything or push buttons they shouldn't.

Sometimes I can sneak in a quick encouraging comment or an invite to a church event, but my brain can't seem to switch off the "how" to just engage with the person in front of me.

Jonah understood who God was calling him to go to, but he got so worked up about the "how" that was required of him, so he plain out just ran away. Right into the belly of a big fish.

"Now the Lord provided a huge fish to swallow Jonah, and Jonah was in the belly of the fish three days and three nights." Jonah 1:17

We cannot run from God no matter how often we run in fear of the call He's given us.

Some of us tie up our sneakers and run, while others of us over-analyze and create a mental excel sheet and graph chart to figure out just how we will fulfill His commands.

Can I share a reminder that God gave me recently through reading this story of Jonah? We don't spend any time living outside of God's provision. So, why do we live like we are on our own when He nudges our hearts towards a certain assignment?

God is in charge of giving us the details as we need them. We are in charge of serving the people He gives us.

If we will make a move towards God each day, He will equip us and shine light on the next step. But it's up to us to make people (not the game plan) our priority. Love God, love people, and stay the course.

Jonah's eventual obedience led to the Ninevites belief in God and ultimately their safety instead of God's original plan to destroy them (3:10).

So the next time you feel the "nudge," focus on the beautiful soul in front of you. Do whatever it takes to show them Jesus and leave your excel sheet behind.

God, redirect our concern in the moments that You need us most. Don't let us get hung up on the details, but help us see the person that You are trying to reach through us. We choose to show up today. We love You. Amen.

41

DUAL INCREASE ELIMINATION

· ·

"When we're concerned with our increase,
we diminish His victory to our vanity."

Michelle Myers

Christian leaders, if there's one verse we all need to be reminded of often, it's the words of John the Baptist, recorded in John 3:30:

"He must increase, but I must decrease."

Because all too often, if we're simply applying business principles to ministry lives, we could falsely believe, "In order to make Him increase, I must increase too."

And sweet friends, that's just not the case. Let's look at deeper context of John's words in John 3:26-30:

And they came to John and said to him, "Rabbi, He who was with you across the Jordan, to whom you bore witness—look, He is baptizing, and all are going to Him." John answered, "A person cannot receive even one thing unless it is given him from Heaven. You yourselves bear me witness, that I said, 'I am not the Christ, but I have been sent before Him.' The one who has the bride is the Bridegroom. The friend of the Bridegroom, who stands and hears Him, rejoices greatly at the Bridegroom's voice. Therefore this joy of mine is now complete. He must increase, but I must decrease."

John the Baptist's followers were worried that it wasn't becoming about John anymore...and he had to remind them that his ministry was never about him in the first place.

The reality is that you may not feel like you've ever attempted to upstage Jesus. But honesty-time:

Are you simply trying to share the stage?

Are you trying to increase…to make Him increase? Or are you actively seeking ways to decrease? Because we can't do both.

There are many routes to destruction, and not all of them exist in the form of simply being "bad." For example, Adrian Rogers once said, "If Satan can't make you bad, he'll make you busy."

By the same token, I'll offer this warning: If Satan can't make you bad, he might try to make you care more about the success of your own legacy than the cause of Christ.

I can't speak for all of us, but I believe the majority of stress among Christian leaders is rooted in the desire of dual increase:

His mission + my mission.

His agenda + my agenda.

His name + my name.

Imagine what it would be like if you were solely focused on His increase alone. Take away all the pressure to be the best, have a larger audience, get more followers…

Would your life look drastically different than it does now?

That's a real question. Answer it out loud. Be honest.

she works His way, we must WAKE UP!

That's not just some dreamy, far-off, wishful thinking. That's exactly how we are supposed to live!

Decrease doesn't mean you disappear. Decrease doesn't mean your life doesn't have meaning. But decrease means we must stop worrying about what role we get to play, and we're just grateful that our story is wrapped up in His.

And because of the life Jesus lived, as vs. 29 says, our joy is complete RIGHT NOW. We're not waiting on full joy to happen if we get to be a big enough part of the story someday.

Bottom line: When we're concerned with our increase, we diminish His victory to our vanity.

And His forever reign is too good to reduce to our temporary gain. Release the dual pressure. Let's decrease, so He can increase.

God, we confess that many times, our flesh is weak, and it's tempting to believe that our increase would help Your cause. But God, You are clear that You take care of us and that You are the Giver of all things. You are our Provider. You are our Hope. God, take away our dual increase desires. Give us an intense desire for Your increase alone. Make us aware when Satan attempts to appeal to our egos. Align us with Your mission, and give us pure hearts as we pursue it solely. We love You. Amen.

42

SPIRIT, SOUL, BODY

. . . .

"His Word is your warfare."

Jessica Hottle

When you said "yes" to Jesus, your spirit totally changed. When you said "yes" to Jesus as your Savior, your spirit had an awakening and a complete transformation.

1 Thessalonians 5:23 tells us that we have three parts: body, soul, and spirit.

"May God himself, the God of peace, sanctify you through and through. May your whole spirit, soul, and body be kept blameless at the coming of our Lord Jesus Christ."

Spirit = Innermost Part
Soul = Mental and Emotional (consisting of mind, will, emotions, conscience. Also, known as your personality.)
Body = Physical Part

The Christian life is not easy. It's not meant to be easy. The battle in our lives is real between the enemy and our one true God. God isn't fighting the enemy. Jesus defeated him at the cross and His resurrection (Romans 6:4-5; Colossians 2:13-15). The battle is between our old man and the new man (Ephesians 4:22-24). You might say it is between our spirit and our soul. The enemy can't touch your soul but he can feed you false truths and deceptions that easily play on your emotions.

Let's look at 2 Corinthians 5:17. It reminds us that we are a new creation.

"This means that anyone who belongs to Christ has become a new person. The old life is gone; a new life has begun!"

When you said "yes" to Jesus, you were made new. We don't get all new things or circumstances - we're made new. But sometimes, things just don't seem to be new in your life at all.

93

Your business is the same.
You find yourself still comparing yourself to others in the industry you are in.
You still second-guess if you are even called to the ministry you are in.
Your bank account hasn't grown.
Your health hasn't gotten better.

The list can go on.

Okay, let me [Jessica] put this all together for you.

If you are in Christ, your spirit has already had a complete transformation. It is – at this moment – perfect, mature, and complete in Jesus. You aren't in the process of trying to get anything from God because He has already made you new.

Now our inner man can be transformed to the degree at which you renew your mind, change your attitudes, and live out (believe) what the Word of God says (2 Corinthians 4:16). It's why Romans 12:2 is so important in our walk with the Lord: ***"Do not conform to the pattern of this world, but be transformed by the renewing of your mind. Then you will be able to test and approve what God's will is—his good, pleasing and perfect will."***

Our inner man doesn't change until the way we think changes by believing God's Word.

James 1:23-25 says, ***"Anyone who listens to the word but does not do what it says is like someone who looks at his face in a mirror and, after looking at himself, goes away and immediately forgets what he looks like. But whoever looks intently into the perfect law that gives freedom, and continues in it— not forgetting what they have heard, but doing it—they will be blessed in what they do."***

The answers you need about how to run your ministry, you already have through His Word.

The questions you have about the decisions you need to make financially or for your family, you already have the wisdom you need through His Word.

Any feelings of insecurities or comparison or doubtfulness, He has already supplied you with the opposite of those things through His Word.

Jesus said "it is finished". He supplied you with everything you need. He didn't forget about you and He knew you would be right where you are today. He is not taken by surprise.

His Word is your warfare.

Father, thank You for choosing me to live out Your will. Thank You for choosing me even though You knew I wouldn't be perfect or get it right all the time. Every day I get to spend with You in Your presence is a gift. Every day I want to look more and more like You, Father. Keep revealing to my soul the truth from Your Word. I love You. Amen!

43

BOLD WORDS

. . . .

"When people hear your name, do they think about
the work you do or the God you serve?"

Emily Copeland

I [Emily] have seen a theme happening for years on social media, and in real life, with Christians. I know this theme all too well because I've allowed it to control me too. The theme is that the results of our work and efforts have become our claim to fame. We aren't afraid to boldly share our accomplishments, but when it comes down to sharing all that God has done in our broken lives to give us success? Crickets.

Do we really believe that the world needs to see more accomplishments? What if they could see more of the God Who can heal their soul and meet their most urgent and eternal needs?

"Salvation is found in no one else, for there is no other name under heaven given to mankind by which we must be saved!" Acts 4:12.

Those are bold words right there! Proclaimed in front of the courts that very well could have condemned them to death, Peter and John stood opposite of a lot of us. They were unschooled and they didn't have the accomplishments to share (or give them credibility) on social media. And I don't think they would have if they could!

What we know about Peter and John from this passage is this:

- They were bold about the message that matters MOST (vs.12)
- They were bold because they had been with Jesus (vs.13)

Peter and John weren't going to change the world with anything other than the gospel of Jesus Christ. They decided not to blend into the crowd, but to stand tall in truth. Their experience in walking with Jesus left them with no other choice but to make Him known, and it should be the same for us.

"...When they saw the courage of Peter and John and realized that they were unschooled, ordinary men, they were astonished and **they took note** *that these men had been with Jesus."* Acts 4:13

When people see you online or at work, what notes are they taking about you? Do they see a girl striving for the typical success of money and growth? Or do they see a girl who has been with Jesus and is determined to make Him known in all that she does?

We can't boldly proclaim truth about a God we are unfamiliar with. Let's dig into His Word today and talk with Him throughout our day. Let's be known as women who have "been with Jesus" and, because of it, others get to meet Him too.

God, forgive us for all of the moments that our story has been about our work and our own name. You are faithful to meet every need even when we don't acknowledge You. We commit to spending time with You today and making You known so that when others hear our name, they think of You. We love You. Amen.

44

DIRECTION

. . . .

"Our faith is on full display when we keep pointing to an
all-knowing God in the midst of our unknown circumstance."

Somer Phoebus

Have you ever been there? A place of knowing that change is coming but without
any idea of what that looks like or when it will happen? You're completely and
totally settled and content, but simultaneously feel a strange anxiousness while
you wait for an inevitable but entirely mysterious "something."

Be encouraged!

If this is you, that means that you are walking with the Lord in an intimate way.
When the Holy Spirit speaks, He is quiet and gentle 99% of the time. So to feel
His presence in this way is to know what it feels like when the God of the universe,
your Creator, grabs you by the shoulders and begins to redirect you toward what
He has for you next. How good is that?

**"And your ears shall hear a word behind you, saying, "This is the way, walk in
it," when you turn to the right or when you turn to the left." Isaiah 30:21**

"My sheep hear my voice, and I know them, and they follow me." John 10:27

**"So faith comes from hearing, and hearing through the word of Christ."
Romans 10:17**

But, if you don't feel this way, if you're UNsettled, DIScontent, and the kind of
anxious that drowns out peace rather than delivers it, there's a disconnect that needs
to be recognized, repented of, and dealt with! You may just be trying to force the
"what's next" in your life and trust me when I [Somer] *(and a large majority of the men
and women we see in the Bible)* tell you that is never a good idea!

**"A man's steps are of the Lord. How then can a man understand his own
way?" Proverbs 20:24**

"There is a way which seems right to a man, but its end is the way of death." **Proverbs 14:12**

"I know, O Lord, that the way of man is not in himself, that it is not in man who walks to direct his steps." **Jeremiah 10:23**

God's Word never promised us our future would be laid out for us to critique. (I'm talking to you, my chronic planner/controller friends!) It's a wonderful thing to feel prepared or ready for what's next, but if you're a believer, it shouldn't take having all the details to feel that way. Being in stride with your Savior should be enough.

An excellent sign that someone is walking with the Lord is how effortless it looks for them to take a step forward in an unknown circumstance. Their faith is on full display as they keep pointing to an all-knowing God in the midst of that unknown circumstance.

We say it all the time, but it truly is ALL about Him, so whether you're settled or unsettled, don't lose sight of what this life is about. It's really never about what's next, or even what's right now. It's about how easy it is for others to identify God moving and working in your life!

God, I want to hear Your voice! Quiet my mind and open up my heart to what it is that You have for me. Help me to be content in my circumstance and full of faith as You lead me. I love You! Amen.

45

CREATED FOR CONNECTION

. . . .

*"As much as we live in a digital world,
God created us for connection and community."*

Liz Patton

Every Fall, we gather together for Narrow, our annual *she works His way* conference. When women share with me what they enjoy most about gathering for Narrow, most of them say they love having the chance to be together face-to-face and heart-to-heart rather than just virtually connecting behind a computer.

I [Liz] would have to agree that meeting one another and being able to fellowship and worship together is my favorite part too. As much as we live in a digital world, God created us for connection and community. We were not just meant to engage on social media posts. Yes, that serves its purpose, but women were meant to *do* life together!

One of my favorite examples of this occurs in the first chapter of Luke, when the Virgin Mary has just been told by the angel, Gabriel, that she will give birth to the Savior of the world. I'm sure that Mary must have felt overwhelmed, confused, and maybe even afraid by this news.

Who does she turn to first after receiving this life-changing news? Not to her mom or her rabbi, but rather her cousin and friend, Elizabeth, who is also miraculously with child. ***"At that time Mary got ready and hurried to a town in the hill country of Judea."* (1:39)** She didn't just get ready—she hurried!

It seems that Mary knew the importance of friendship. Whether you're coming to Narrow or just have a desire to foster rich friendships in your life, I think there are three things we can take away from the relationship between Elizabeth and Mary.

1. Friends are like-minded and affirm each other.
The journey that Mary traveled to visit Elizabeth was about 80 to 100 miles and would probably have taken Mary three to four days to walk there. Y'all know she must have been desperate for connection with Elizabeth to make that hard, long

journey (while carrying the Messiah in her belly, no less!).

As soon as she entered the home of Elizabeth and Zechariah, ***"Elizabeth was filled with the Holy Spirit. In a loud voice she exclaimed: "Blessed are you among women, and blessed is the child you will bear!"*** (1:41-42).

I just love picturing Elizabeth loudly affirming Mary! Imagine the hope this brought Mary to know that God had revealed to Elizabeth that she was going to give birth to Jesus. That she didn't just dream up this whole thing, and that she wasn't alone.

The same is true of our friendships today, ladies! We need like-minded women who "get" us to call out what they see in us, to encourage us to pursue what God has laid on our hearts, and to come alongside us so we don't have to journey alone.

2. **Friends don't compete; they celebrate.**
The other fascinating thing about the friendship of Elizabeth and Mary is that there was no jealousy or competition between them. Imagine how excited Elizabeth was about HER miracle, about HER pregnancy. I mean she waited a looooong time to finally become a mama! And then young, teenaged Mary comes on the scene with her pregnancy announcement. And rather than be jealous or bitter, Elizabeth rejoices with her! ***"But why am I so favored, that the mother of my Lord should come to me?"*** (1:43) Not one ounce of jealousy - just humility and love.

Oh, sisters! May this be an example to us! There is no need for us to compete with each other. Her success is not your failure. There is room enough for all of us, and we need to spend the short amount of time we have here on earth encouraging each other and celebrating one another's accomplishments!

3. **Friends encourage each other.**
Mary's visit lasted for about three months, which would have been for the duration of Elizabeth's pregnancy. Can't you just picture these two women sharing in their pregnancies and miracles together? I also imagine that Elizabeth was encouraging, loving, and praying over Mary so that when Mary did return home – where she would probably be subject to taunting and gossip – she could endure it.

Maybe you aren't able to join us at Narrow this year, but I still want to encourage you to find a way this week to be available for a friend *(other than on social media)* to offer her some encouragement. I know our schedules are all super busy, and it's so easy to hide behind our computers and play it safe. But we'll never regret meeting a friend to affirm her, to celebrate her, and to encourage her, with our whole hearts. Now let's get ready and do some "hurrying" of our own!

Dear God, thank You that You created us for connection. Thank You for knitting our hearts together with like-minded women. Stir us and equip us to go outside of our comfort zones to be available for our friends. Give us the words and actions to affirm, celebrate, and encourage the women in our lives so that they can be all that You have created them to be. For those of us attending Narrow, we are so expectant for You, Lord. We can't wait for You to show up and show off for us. Come, Lord Jesus, come. We love You. Amen.

I AM

. . . .

"Every word you speak is bringing life or death to your business."

Jessica Hottle

After God told Moses that he was going to be leading His people out of Egypt, we see a dialogue between a Father and a son who feels less than qualified to do the job.

Moses tries to convince God that He has the wrong man.

Just like anyone would probably ask when leading a whole nation out of captivity, Moses says, "Suppose I get to the Israelites and say to them, 'The God of your fathers has sent me to you,' and they ask me, 'What is his name?' Then what shall I tell them?"

God's response is in Exodus 3:14: **"I AM WHO I AM. This is what you are to say to the Israelites: 'I AM has sent me to you.'"**

He is God. But, He is also I AM.

In business, it's easy to get lost in what we aren't doing, the results we wish we could be creating, and the lack of followers we wish we had.

Therefore, this leads us to our own I AM statements. It's important to really understand that the words you speak either bring life or death. (See Proverbs 18:21.)

Maybe you have never thought of it this way before, but Scripture tells us to not use God's name in vain. We see that in Exodus 20:7, **"You shall not take the name of the LORD your God in vain, for the LORD will not hold him guiltless who takes His name in vain."**

If God is also I AM, then I believe the words that follow our "I ams" need to match the Father's heart and nature. (Speaking life!)
If what we speak brings life or death, then the words we choose showcase the

God (or god) we are choosing to serve.

No one is going to get it perfectly. (I know I [Jessica] don't!) But, this can make us slow down, breathe, and think about the thoughts we are thinking and saying to ourselves, about ourselves, and to others.

The question I pose to you today is this: Does your "I am" match the I AM's heart and nature?

Maybe you have said to yourself...

I am not smart enough.
I am not good enough.
I am not successful.
I am poor.

We can't live by our senses and live by the Spirit at the same time.

If we are only operating by what we see, feel, touch, smell, and hear, then those conclusions might ring true.

But since we don't operate by our senses but by the Spirit, the statements above will look different.

Let's start repeating these *I am* statements over ourselves:

I am gifted: ***"For God's gifts and his call are irrevocable."*** **Romans 11:29**

I am enough: ***"For we are his workmanship, created in Christ Jesus for good works, which God prepared beforehand, that we should walk in them."*** **Ephesians 2:10**

I am equipped with what I need: ***"For the LORD your God has blessed you in all that you have done; He has known your wanderings through this great wilderness These forty years the LORD your God has been with you; you have not lacked a thing."'*** **Deuteronomy 2:7** (If God provided everything the Israelites needed for 40 years, then be encouraged, because He's doing the same thing for you.)

I am wealthy in Christ: ***"And my God will meet all your needs according to his glorious riches in Christ Jesus."*** **Philippians 4:9**

Spend time with Him today and journal through your "I am" statements that you often say to yourself. Then replace them with the true I AM.

Let this be our prayer for today: ***Father, let Your I AM be my I am. Amen!***

47

THE GOOD LIFE

"Rather than learning to defend our position well, we are called to love and serve those who don't stand in our position."

Emily Copeland

It's no secret. Our world is a little divided. It doesn't take more than a minute of scrolling social media to see it. And, it doesn't take more than a minute of watching any news station (or comedy show for that matter) to see that most people stand firm in a certain position.

Being an eloquent, graceful, and firm voice to make an impact is becoming more of a thing of the past. What is the language that speaks louder than words in today's culture? Action.

As women who lead, we have to understand the implications of this verse:

"Live such good lives among the pagans that, though they accuse you of doing wrong, they may see your good deeds and glorify God on the day He visits us." 1 Peter 2:12

Women of influence, hear me [Emily] say this: The good life that Peter is speaking of is not a result of arguing our beliefs or defending our position well. The good life = Loving and serving those who don't stand in our position.

Will we be accused of doing wrong or believing in the wrong thing? Probably. Does it give us ground to shame, ignore, belittle or think less of other people? Definitely not. We have the ability to live such good lives of love and service (beyond what we really feel in any given moment), that unbelievers can see the glory of God in our lives.

"...they may see your good deeds and glorify God on the day He visits us."

Before you step out into public or hop on social media, invite God into your day. Ask Him to give you opportunities to live the good life that Peter talks about.

Remember that we are here, in this century, to live out God's purpose not to just defend it. What we do with the time we've been given matters. Lifting others up instead of tearing them down in the name of a debate will hinder the mission, not help it.

Be the business owner who operates with such integrity that people see a difference in what you do. Be a stay-at-home momma who teaches servanthood as a most important characteristic. Be a woman in the corporate world who sees every coworker as a part of the mission. Live out loud with an undeniable love because judgment is God's job.

We sure love journeying with you, sister!

God, thank You for putting us here in this season. We pray that we won't just make a shallow imprint, but that we would make a lasting impact for the kingdom. May our voice be strong, but our actions be louder. Open our eyes to see the people who need Your love the most. We want to live the good life because it's exactly what we're here to do. We love You. Amen

48

MOVED AND MOTIVATED

· ·

"Forgiveness isn't just our responsibility; it's our opportunity."

Somer Phoebus

I [Somer] love the story of Joseph and that bright, beautiful coat of his. *(If you've not read this Bible story, I would encourage you to go read it! Begin in Genesis 37, and finish out the book.)*

As I read this story recently, I was moved and motivated once again by Joseph's response to the unfair treatment he received from his brothers.

Side note: That's exactly what reading God's Word should do for us. We should be moved and motivated!

Joseph's father, Jacob, was pretty open about the fact that Joseph was his favorite. He showed him (and everyone else) his favoritism by gifting Joseph the famous multicolored coat. Because of that, Joseph was hated by his brothers. I mean, HATED.

Through a series of events and the scheming of those wicked brothers, *(there were 11 of them!)* Joseph found himself sold into slavery to the Egyptians.

Then through another series of events and the blessing of God, Joseph then found himself as second in command over Egypt.

Yes, Joseph went from slave boy to second in command over an entire nation. Only God, my friends!

But then we get to the part of the story I'd like to focus on today. The part where Joseph proves he loves God more than he loves his own desires. The part that should move and motivate us to be more like Joseph.

There was a seven-year famine, and very quickly into that famine, Joseph's brothers ran out of food. In fear for their lives and the lives of their families, they took off to Egypt to see if they could find what they needed there. Egypt was the only place where there wasn't a shortage of grain, thanks to Joseph listening to God and storing up heaps of grain seven years prior to the drought.

When the brothers reached Egypt to buy food, they didn't recognize that the man they were buying it from was their brother, Joseph. But Joseph knew exactly who they were.

Instead of turning them away or throwing them in jail, Joseph had mercy on his family and gave them food. He even returned their money.

Joseph loved his brothers the way God loved Joseph.

Friend, you may be hurting in a big way today. I would beg you to do business with God this morning and go where it's not fun to go. Your hurt may be old, it may be buried, or it might be so fresh that this is already stinging.

No matter what it is, be like Joseph, and love those who hurt you! Do you understand that your very act of love, when it is not deserved, could be the loudest, most attention-grabbing thing to demonstrate God's love to the person who wronged you?

Forgiveness isn't just our responsibility; it's our opportunity!

Today, let Scripture move and motivate you to do whatever it is that God wants you to do. If it's forgiveness, forgive! If it's obedience in an area of your life you've been fighting to hold onto – surrender it and obey. I want the relationship that Joseph had with his Heavenly Father, but that means I have to actively pursue it. Will you pursue it too?

God, thank You for Your Word and the way it is so incredibly applicable to where I am today, so many years later. Please open my heart to forgiveness, pull me out of the sin I am in, and let me be totally and completely surrendered to You! I love You. Amen.

49

I CANNOT GO DOWN

. . . .

"Lord, help me to be able to say 'No' to the good projects so
I can say 'Yes' to the great ones."

Liz Patton

"I am carrying on a great project and cannot go down. Why should the work stop while I leave it and go down to you?" Nehemiah 6:3

If you're not familiar with the story of Nehemiah, I [Liz] want to encourage you to read it in its entirety, because there are so many great takeaways that are applicable to us as *she works His way* women.

What jumps out to me about verse 6:3 – and one of the things I love most about Nehemiah – is that he recognizes what he is doing is a "great project." Not because he is being boastful or arrogant, but rather because Nehemiah knows that God Himself put this project on his heart (Nehemiah 2:12).

And because this is a special calling from God, Nehemiah is not willing to lose focus or stop working. Even though he has been lured away FOUR different times by these wicked schemers, he remains persistent and dedicated.

I also love that he doesn't feel the need to please others. He knows this is what God has laid on his heart. He trusts that the God of Heaven will bring him success, so his blinders are on, and he is Kingdom-focused. As Sandra Stanley puts it in her book, *Breathing Room*, "*sometimes a simple no or not right now to someone in our outer circle can have a huge impact on someone in our inner circle.*"

Quite honestly, this both convicts and inspires me at the same time. I know that I know that I know that my "great project" right now is being a wife and Mama. Yes, I feel called to my business, and I'm passionate about it, but I have had to give myself permission to be ordinary in my business so that I can be extraordinary in my great project. I have to constantly remind myself that I "cannot go down" right now.

Please hear my heart, that doesn't mean that I blow off everything else. I still want to be a good steward and do my work with excellence just as it says in **Colossians 3:23: *"Whatever you do, do it from the heart, as something done for the Lord and not for people."*** But what it does mean is that I've had to go at a slower pace. For example, when I write my goals, I no longer have a due date for their completion; I no longer have to serve on every single committee; and it's okay sometimes to send in paper plates instead of gourmet cupcakes for the class party.

The world is good at making us think that we have to be the best at all. the. things. But you know what? God doesn't ask us to be great at everything. Like Nehemiah, let's identify our "great project" and make that our focus. Because <spoiler alert>…if you continue reading in Nehemiah's story, you'll see that when his enemies heard about his success in re-building the wall, ***"they realized that this work had been done with the help of our God."*** And wouldn't that be the greatest success of all?

Dear God, thank You for giving me the great projects that are in my life. Help me to have the courage to be different from the rest of the world and to be able to say "no" to the good things so I can say "yes" to the great things. Thank You for putting Your gracious hand upon me. I love You with all my heart. Amen.

50

FEED MY SHEEP

. . . .

"Rather than clinging to an '*I love Jesus, but I...*' *life*,
we must lead an, '*I love Jesus, SO I...*' *life*."

Michelle Myers

There's a growing trend to be a student of yourself. And while there's definitely wisdom in being self-aware, when it comes to delving into in-depth studies of our personality tendencies and quirks, can we all admit that probably the last thing any of us *really* needs is to feed our fleshly bent toward selfishness?

Just look around. The next time you're at a restaurant, track how long it takes you to find someone without his or her face buried in a phone. I [Michelle] would say the majority of people today use most of our spare moments to scroll...not to open our eyes to the needs around us.

Let's read Ezekiel's warning to the leaders in Israel:

"Woe, shepherds of Israel who have been feeding themselves! Should not the shepherds feed the flock? You eat the fat and clothe yourselves with the wool, you slaughter the fat sheep without feeding the flock. Those who are sickly you have not strengthened, the diseased you have not healed, the broken you have not bound up, the scattered you have not brought back, nor have you sought for the lost; but with force and severity you have dominated them..." Ezekiel 34:2b-4

As I was reading, I couldn't help but think of the conversation recorded in John 21 between Jesus and Peter, where three times, Jesus asked him, "Simon Peter, do you love me?" And after he replied "yes" each time, Jesus followed Peter's professed love for Him with a charge:

"Tend my lambs." (v. 15)

"Take care of my sheep." (v. 16)

"Feed my sheep." (v. 17)

Jesus put it bluntly, but they were both saying the same thing: Loving Jesus motivates us to take action on the behalf of others – not ourselves.

Sadly, this is not the growing "gospel" we often see today. It's much more common to see the, "I love Jesus but I [fill in the blank]" message.

And while it's intended to be cute, clever, or even poke at the very real idea that we aren't perfect, at its core it says, "I love Jesus, but I can still choose to do what I want."

she works His way, that's not the life we're called to live, especially if we lead.

Rather than clinging to an "I love Jesus, but I..." life, we must lead an, "I love Jesus, SO I..." life.

So I...search out the lost (Ezekiel 34:11-16).

So I...strengthen the weak (Ezekiel 34:16).

So I...gather the dispersed (Ezekiel 34:13).

So I...bind up the hurting (Ezekiel 34:16).

So I...feed the hungry (Ezekiel 34:13).

Plain and simple: Genuine, godly leadership, motivated by love for Jesus, focuses on serving others.

Not getting ahead.

Not justifying our selfishness.

Not satisfying our flesh.

Ezekiel put it this way: **"My shepherds did not search for My flock, but rather the shepherds fed themselves and did not feed my flock" Ezekiel 34:8b.**

I don't know about you, but when Jesus looks down at me, I don't want Him to see a fat sheep, but a steady chef. And it takes a lot more effort to cook in the kitchen than simply to eat at the table.

Will you do me a favor today? You can share it with me if you'd like, but just between you and Jesus, would you write down your own "so I" statement today? Just simply write it out as a prayer and a promise between you and Him:

"I love Jesus, so I _____."

Then...let's get cooking. :)

God, thank You for Your Word that is always on time and always what our souls need. God, each day, I have to make the choice to walk in Your Spirit rather than feed my flesh. Don't let me fall for the world's schemes, no matter how clever or harmless they may seem. My desire is for my love for You to flow into a "so I" life, not a "but I" life. But I need Your strength to work in me first, so You can work through me. I love You. Make my life show it. Amen.

51

THE ONE

. . . .

"No matter how many titles you have behind your name,
you come to a point when you realize you can't do it alone.
It's not about you, and that the mission He has you on
is so much bigger than the title you think you need."

Jessica Hottle

I [Jessica] remember trying to do it all.

I wanted every title behind my name that I could have, because, the more titles
I had, the more I thought others would take me seriously, think I was successful,
and know my name.

Maybe you don't know my story or know me at all (Hi, it's nice to meet you!), but
I didn't know the Lord until I was about 21. Before I was saved, I knew nothing
about God. I didn't understand why Jesus and God were different. Weren't
they the same? Who was Jesus? Why were people saying they were Catholic or
Christian or went to a non-denominational church versus a Baptist church? What
did it all mean?

To be honest. It was overwhelming. I felt stupid.

I felt stupid raising my hands in church and singing. So, I stood there with my
arms folded down in front of me.

I tithed, somewhat, because I heard it was a good thing to do. It wasn't consistent
by any means and it for sure wasn't my first fruits.

It took me a few years to steadily read the Bible on a consistent basis, without
just picking out some encouraging verses here and there, and another few years
to begin to live out what those verses meant. I would share Jesus on social media,
but I wasn't living it behind the scenes.

Although time has passed since I met Jesus, I would say that the last 3-4 years are really when I began my true walk with Him in friendship and seeing God as my Father.

Why am I sharing this with you?

The work you are doing today is helping people, like the me at 21, who never entered a church and didn't know who Jesus is.

The work you do matters and the disciples recognized the importance of this kind of work in Acts 6:1-7.

The church was growing and they realized that they needed to be on the mission field, not serving tables because the *"Hellenists (Greek-speaking Jews) believed that their widows were being neglected in the daily distribution"* (v. 1-2).

So, they called a meeting to *"raise up seven leaders who were honorable, full of the Spirit, and wisdom"* (v. 3).

The raising up of other leaders resulted in helping the Word of God continue to increase and the *"number of disciples multiplied greatly in Jerusalem and a great many of the priests became obedient to the faith"* (v. 7).

No matter how many titles you have behind your name, you come to a point when you realize you can't do it alone, it's not about you, and that the mission He has you on is so much bigger than the title you think you need.

Here's the questions to ask yourself today:

- How are you reaching the one who may not know Jesus today?

- How are you reaching the one who may know Jesus as their Savior but needs to grow in His Truth?

Father, I'd be nothing without You. Let me stand in the humility that tells me it's all about You and not about me. I love You! Amen!

52

GODLINESS + CONTENTMENT

. . . .

"Only other broken and flawed human beings have said
that riches and success in life will make you better."

Emily Copeland

***"But godliness with contentment is great gain."* 1 Timothy 6:6**

I [Emily] am not sure that most people can read that verse without giving a
metaphorical fist pump in the air. (Am I alone in this?!) This verse feels like a win
and I know that we all want a win. But this verse wasn't written because it's simple
and easy to walk in contentment and godliness all of the time. This verse calls us
to something higher than we are used to, but with God, it is totally possible.

As women pursuing Jesus in our work and in our homes, we cannot escape the
reality that money is important to us. Some of us are comfortable with little, while
others of us live for more and more of it. The phrase "godliness with contentment"
means adding nothing else to what you have and being 100% ok with it.

We don't live in a world where just having food and clothing is enough. It has to
be the RIGHT food and the RIGHT clothing, and forget about having just enough
of it. We must have extras just in case (my legging collection is pretty fierce, I
cannot lie).

In our work, we have great influence over others in the area of living in
contentment and walking in godliness. So I must ask, how are we currently
promoting contentment to others? Do we talk about our work and hope to
inspire others with the benefits of a successful lifestyle? Do we tell people to
work for their dreams more than we encourage them to be content right where
they are?

One of the most universally accepted messages out there is that financial success
is worth fighting for. And most of us have climbed aboard this train. We talk
about how "freeing" this success is and we talk about how to get there and how
to gain more. We also talk about how much money has changed our life. But, are

we clouding our mission's message by doing so? Does a public attempt to be financially successful cloud our public message about Jesus?

Only other broken and flawed human beings have said that riches and success in life will make you better. You can't find Jesus making that statement in the Bible. In fact, Jesus says, **"Then he said to them, 'Watch out! Be on your guard against all kinds of greed; life does not consist in an abundance of possessions.'" Luke 12:15**

Here is the reality: People can easily get on board with your message about making money. So will you take the easy route to promote financial success as your main message? Or, will you show them that following Jesus is the greatest treasure?

Even if you gain wealth through hard work, Paul tells us in 1 Timothy 6:17 that we cannot put our hope in our wealth. He says, **"Command those who are rich in this present world not to be arrogant nor to put their hope in wealth, which is so uncertain, but to put their hope in God, who richly provides us with everything for our enjoyment."**

Instead, **"Fight the good fight of the faith. Take hold of the eternal life to which you were called when you made your good confession in the presence of many witnesses." (v. 12)**

Living in godliness and contentment in what we have is not to hold us back from anything good. Rather, it frees us up to truly live our best life.

Check this out: **"In this way they will lay up treasure for themselves as a firm foundation for the coming age, so that they may take hold of the life that is truly life." (v. 19)**

If you've walked with God for any amount of time, you know that His promises are pretty life-altering and not one has fallen through the cracks. So, we can trust Him in this promise too. Pursuing wealth and making it our main message to the world can only lead to emptiness. It's ultimately the opposite of living a life of contentment. Money is a providential gift from God, not a symbol of our status or worth. Let's choose to begin bringing God into this area of our lives so that He can make His mark and remind us that He is more than enough. Then, let's take this message to our world: Money is a gift, Jesus is the treasure.

God, You've seen money supply needs but You've also watched it destroy the lives of people whom You love. Help us to see money for what it is and to pursue contentment and godliness because we have everything that we need in You alone. Help us to recognize this so that we can live our life that is truly LIFE today and every day. We love You. Amen.

53

EMBRACE THE PAIN

. . . .

"Don't run from your pain! Run towards your Comforter!"

Somer Phoebus

I [Somer] was recently on a trip with Kent in beautiful California. During some free time, I visited a new gym that I had never heard of and I loved it! But I think the reason I loved it was more about the super welcoming and incredibly dynamic trainer and not so much the actual workout.

Let me tell you, this girl was ON! From the second I walked into her workout room until we finished the final rep, she was dynamic, full of energy, and hilarious! But then came the cool down.

Immediately, the lights came down, the music changed, and so did our trainer. Her voice was soft and, instead of yelling at me, all of the sudden she was speaking in the most soothing tone. I mean it was like a different person had entered the room!

I couldn't help but smile at her words, knowing that my God was speaking right to me in the middle of this gym I had never been in and through a trainer I had never met. It was pretty clear she wasn't a believer, so I'm sure she had no idea why I had such a cheesy grin but, boy, was it sweet.

She said several things that reminded me of God's goodness, but one thing in particular stood out…

the word PAIN.

During the beginning of the workout, she asked us to embrace the pain.

In the middle of the workout, she reminded us why the pain was worth it.

At the end of the workout, she showed us how to relieve our pain so we could move past it.

Do I even need to explain this analogy? This girl was basically preaching Romans 5:3-5, which was EXACTLY what I needed to hear at that very moment:

"Not only that, but we rejoice in our sufferings, knowing that suffering produces endurance, and endurance produces character, and character produces hope, and hope does not put us to shame, because God's love has been poured into our hearts through the Holy Spirit who has been given to us." Romans 5:3-5

Are you at the beginning of your pain? God asks us to rejoice in it, to embrace it. I remember a very dark time in our lives where I thought my pain was for nothing, but looking back now I wouldn't trade those days for the world. God says in this life there will be suffering. We don't need to fight it, or to try to hide from it. Instead, we need to know Who to turn to when it comes!

"I have told you these things, so that in me you may have peace. In this world you will have trouble. But take heart! I have overcome the world." John 16:33

Are you in the middle of your pain? You need to be reminded that this pain is so worth it. That everyday gone is one day closer to eternity with our Heavenly Father, so while we're here on earth, we can't let this vapor of time be about our happiness. We have to make it about His holiness. We can't make it about our comfort. We have to make it about His Kingdom!

"...yet you do not know what tomorrow will bring. What is your life? For you are a mist that appears for a little time and then vanishes." James 4:14

If you're in a season of suffering will you let me (and Scripture) remind you that this is exactly par for the course as a follower of Jesus? If you're a believer, there will be trials, but that's when we're able to show Him off in the biggest way!

Don't run from your pain! Run towards your Comforter! He's got you, friend!

Dear God, I am so sorry that I take You for granted. Thank You for saving me and for dying on the cross so that I could suffer for Your most wonderful name! God, I pray that You would give me the strength to embrace the pain and to walk in You the whole way! I can't wait to see what You do through me. Thank You for holding me so that I'm never alone. I love You. Amen.

54

SPIRITUAL GROWTH

. . . .

"As Christians, there is a time for us to be in our Father's nest
- a time to learn, grow, and be covered with His feathers. But then,
as we grow and mature in our faith, it's time for us to leave the nest."

Liz Patton

For the last few years, we've had a mama bird build a nest in the wreath on our front door, lay her eggs, and then care for her baby birds until they leave the nest. Quite honestly, I [Liz] have never been a big fan of birds; They just seem kind of unpredictable, like they want to fly into my head or poop on me! But ever since watching this mama bird do her thing, I have to admit that I've gotten a bit attached to them.

I don't know how accurate this is, but I recently heard that the mama bird builds her nest first with prickly twigs and objects before filling it with softer leaves, grass, or twigs. This is done purposefully because she doesn't want the baby birds to get too comfortable after they hatch. She eventually wants them to leave the nest, fly away, and become independent.

As Christians, there is a time for us to be in our Father's nest. A time to learn, grow, and be covered with His feathers:

"He will cover you with his feathers, and under his wings you will find refuge; his faithfulness will be your shield and rampart." Psalm 91:4

But then as we grow and mature in our faith – like the baby birds – it's time for us to leave the nest!

"So put away all malice and all deceit and hypocrisy and envy and all slander. Like newborn infants, long for the pure spiritual milk, that by it you may grow up into salvation— if indeed you have tasted that the Lord is good. As you come to him, a living stone rejected by men but in the sight of God chosen and precious, you yourselves like living stones are being built up

120

as a spiritual house, to be a holy priesthood, to offer spiritual sacrifices acceptable to God through Jesus Christ." 1 Peter 2:1-5

If we are the same women next year as we are today, we're not growing or preparing to leave the nest. Like a newborn, we need to crave God's Word like pure spiritual milk! And as we continue to drink from our Bibles, and taste that the Lord is good, we will grow stronger so that we can offer ourselves as spiritual sacrifices to our Heavenly Father!

As we pursue growing in our faith, it's sometimes easy to rely on man to interpret God's Word for us. I'm not saying that we shouldn't do Bible studies, read the study notes in our Bibles, or do Google searches to learn more. However, if we are relying on those resources more than on God Himself, we won't truly grow.

I encourage you to pray before reading God's Word and ask Him to reveal new truths to you! Let Him know the desire of your heart to grow in your relationship with Him so that you can be built up as His spiritual house. You are chosen and precious, and your Father wants to help you grow. Let's seek Him above all else!

Dear God, I love being covered by Your feathers and taking refuge under the shadow of Your wings. But Lord, I know You want to strengthen me so that I'm able to fly! As I read Your Word, speak to my heart and reveal new truths to me so that I may grow in my relationship with You. I love You. Amen.

55

FAMILY IS FAMILY

. . . .

"Believers only lose our unity when something has
become more important than Jesus."

Michelle Myers

Holidays mean there's a reason to celebrate...but for many, holidays bring a mix
of emotions.

Holidays often create large gatherings with family, and depending on the home
you grew up in (or perhaps married into), those get-togethers can add layer upon
layer of emotions, differences, and difficulty.

But at the end of the day, no matter what challenges arise, you can't change your
family, can you? So rather than just running off to find another family, most of the
time, we cling together and love one another, despite the imperfections.

Why? Because that's what families do.

But let me [Michelle] ask you a real question: Do you have the same commitment
to your spiritual family?

We should. Let's look at Matthew 12:46-50 together:

**"While Jesus was still talking to the crowd, his mother and brothers stood
outside, wanting to speak to him. Someone told him, "Your mother and
brothers are standing outside, wanting to speak to you." He replied to him,
"Who is my mother, and who are my brothers?" Pointing to his disciples, he
said, "Here are my mother and my brothers. For whoever does the will of my
Father in heaven is my brother and sister and mother."**

Now, Jesus was not dismissing the value of his earthly relationships. In fact, on
the cross, some of the last words Jesus spoke were instructions to John to care
for his mother, Mary (John 19:25-27).

But Jesus' point here is to ensure that we view our spiritual relationships the same way we view our earthly relationships:

Mandatory.

Irrevocable.

Unalterable.

Do we live in that kind of unity with other believers?

And I'm not talking about just our close circle of Christian friends. I'm talking about every single person who confesses Christ.

I'll answer: We don't.

We let worldly factors creep into how we treat one another. We decide to disassociate with one another because of politics, personal interests, or socioeconomic statuses. We can let one argument fester into a forever feud. Or we can simply let fear of the unknown stop us from desiring to get to know one another.

Total truth time?

Believers only lose our unity when something has become more important than Jesus.

Plain and simple.

If we want a lost world to notice something different, we have to live differently. And if we choose to live in the same divisions that everyone outside our spiritual family lives in, that's not an effective witness to a world that *is* watching and desperately wants a solution for their empty lives.

Several months ago, my pastor put it something like this: "The church shouldn't be full of a bunch of people who love each other because they look alike, talk alike, and think alike. The church should be full of people so different that there is no explanation for why they love each other except for the fact that they have Jesus in common."

So just like you put up with that crazy cousin because "family is family," spiritually, we need to have that same commitment because Jesus is Jesus.

I think we'd all agree that, if we agree on Jesus, that's all that really matters. So can we drop the other labels, the other qualifiers to be friends?

The world pays attention to unity. Unity may be hard to define, but it's impossible to miss.

Let's give them something to see.

God, thank You for sending Jesus as a clear example for how we are to live our lives. God, we need Your perspective. Help us to see our Christian brothers and sisters as You see them. Give us a passion to be unified. Give us a commitment to live in such radical unity that the watching world can't help but pay attention. Create curiosity in the hearts of those around us for the gospel, Lord. Convict us when we pursue anything less than unity that points to You. We love You. Amen.

56

WHEN BAD THINGS HAPPEN TO GOOD LEADERS

. . . .

"Our job is to focus on the work He has for us, not the outcome!"

Somer Phoebus

This past November, we walked through a lot of Nehemiah in our *she works His way* classes. I [Somer] was able to dig into this book of the Bible that I have always loved so much, and the takeaways were incredible. But one in particular stood out to me this time.

Nehemiah is known for his leadership skills – that's exactly why so many churches and Christian organizations teach Nehemiah when they're looking to develop leaders. He was bold. He was resilient. He was respected. And, most of all, he trusted that God had his back! But, as I highlighted in my class, "The Active Leader," Nehemiah didn't get to bask in the glory of his hard work after the wall was built. Quite the contrary. And we often forget to tell that part of the story.

If you read Nehemiah, you will notice that the first 12 chapters are about a man who saw a need, became burdened for his people, was immediately motivated to action, and was confident in his God. So Nehemiah went and rebuilt the walls of Jerusalem that had been destroyed. Nehemiah was challenged in a multitude of ways but he persevered and he did it. The walls were rebuilt!

Happy ending, right?

Wrong.

About halfway through chapter 12 (the book is only 13 chapters long), things begin to change as we start to see God's people once again blatantly disobeying His Law. These were the same people that Nehemiah worked with day-in and day-out. The people that stood together broken-hearted and confessed their sin after listening to Ezra read the Law in chapter 9.

After the wall was finished, Nehemiah had gone back to work for the king, but then decided to check in on the work he had been part of and the people he

125

loved so much. So he went back to Jerusalem and what he found was not good! Here's what Nehemiah 13:6-14 says:

"While this was taking place, I was not in Jerusalem, for in the thirty-second year of Artaxerxes king of Babylon I went to the king. And after some time I asked leave of the king and came to Jerusalem, and I then discovered the evil that Eliashib had done for Tobiah, preparing for him a chamber in the courts of the house of God. And I was very angry, and I threw all the household furniture of Tobiah out of the chamber. Then I gave orders, and they cleansed the chambers, and I brought back there the vessels of the house of God, with the grain offering and the frankincense. I also found out that the portions of the Levites had not been given to them, so that the Levites and the singers, who did the work, had fled each to his field. So I confronted the officials and said, "Why is the house of God forsaken?" And I gathered them together and set them in their stations. Then all Judah brought the tithe of the grain, wine, and oil into the storehouses. And I appointed as treasurers over the storehouses Shelemiah the priest, Zadok the scribe, and Pedaiah of the Levites, and as their assistant Hanan the son of Zaccur, son of Mattaniah, for they were considered reliable, and their duty was to distribute to their brothers. Remember me, O my God, concerning this, and do not wipe out my good deeds that I have done for the house of my God and for his service."

So why did this pretty disappointing and anti-climactic ending to Nehemiah preach so much to me? Because leaders are always teaching other leaders how to be "successful," but we forget to remind each other that it doesn't always end with success. EVEN WHEN WE DO EVERYTHING RIGHT, the outcome can be a disappointment. Nehemiah did everything God asked of him and God protected him and blessed his work. But because there was a sin issue in the hearts of the people, evil was still present.

What if God had just ended Nehemiah after chapter 11? Wouldn't that have been so much better? We could have cheered for Nehemiah and felt so good about the results of his work. It would have been motivating, inspiring, and the happily ever after that we all desire in a great story.

But then we'd miss this incredible lesson. The Bible is real; it isn't a fairytale. And it wasn't written to entertain us – it was written to teach us.

Nehemiah 12b-13 taught me that God is good and that His plan is perfect. Because of that, I can't give up or grow weary in doing what He's called me to just because the outcome isn't what I had hoped for. I can't control people...I can barely manage my own life!

But I know Who can and I know that, even when it feels like my blood, sweat, and tears have not produced a big, beautiful, thriving crop, it doesn't mean that my work is insignificant...and it doesn't mean that I'm allowed to give up.

Be encouraged today! Your job is to focus on the work He has for you, not the outcome!

Dear God, have I been obedient to what You've asked of me? Please forgive me for the times I haven't. Please help me to focus on the work You have for my hands instead of the outcome! Give me energy to not give up and strength to do my best for You. I love You! Amen.

57

SKILLED

. . . .

*"Being skilled in your work does not mean
that it's okay to wear yourself out to get rich."*

Emily Copeland

Have you ever been guilty of going "all-in" with an opportunity because it allowed you to use your gifts, talents, and natural abilities? What is so awesome about God is that He entrusts each of us with a very personalized skill set. But in human fashion, we are, at times, guilty of taking the good and running in our own direction with it.

Here are a few indications that you may have experienced this before:
- You stop hanging out with or connecting with certain friends who don't understand your calling.

- You're guilty of saying, "I have to do this because God has gifted *only me* to make it happen."

- You're guilty of thinking, "God will surely bless us financially since I've given up many things to give Him the best of my talents and skill."

One small thing that I personally forgot along the way…God doesn't gift us with talent to bless us. Our skills are given so that we can give them right back to God. They are not a tool for our own personal use and they are especially not given to be a means of a big ol' paycheck or greater applause. God has far better things to lavish on us than money or fame.

Proverbs 22:29 gives us a glance into the importance of using the skills that God has given us: ***"Do you see someone skilled in their work? They will serve before kings."***

But very quickly, we see the big stop sign appear just a couple of verses later in Proverbs 23:4, ***"Do not wear yourself out to get rich; do not trust your own cleverness."***

We can't use our God-given abilities as an excuse to stay in the rat race or to pursue a comfortable, cushy life. If God provides wealth, wonderful, but don't you dare count on it or make it the goal. The enemy would be so thrilled! We give our talents and abilities back to God as an offering of praise and thanks because HE deserves it, not because we do.

Let's lay out a new plan today – and don't be afraid to spend some time in repentance if you've wandered into the rat race and forgotten to include God, Who has provided it all, in it.

1. *Identify your God-given skills*

2. *Include Him at the beginning of your work day (Be in His Word + Pray)*

3. *Lay down your own success plan*

4. *Praise Him for the gifts*

5. *Ask that He use them through you for His glory, not yours*

God can do infinitely more with the skills He's given us than we could ever fathom of doing on our own. Work hard, work with integrity and excellence, and keep pointing the success back to Him.

God, You know our hearts and how easily distracted we can be. Help us to recognize the specific skill sets You've blessed us with and break our hearts for what breaks Yours. May we never misuse what You've given us. Thank You for Your faithfulness and make us bold for the Kingdom! We love You. Amen.

58

THE 98%

. . . .

*"It's the things we do that no one sees that make
the greatest impact in the Kingdom."*

Jessica Hottle

Congrats, you are the top 2% in your company. It shows you are dedicated, consistent, hardworking, and driven.

You have achieved a high honor. You have received awards, bonuses, and maybe even some recognition.

Not in the top 2% of your company? No worries. That's not what today is about anyways.

Being in the top 2% of anything isn't bad. It's the chase and the race to get there that I [Jessica] want to talk about.

What I have noticed about success in the many years of being in business is that we are told to do whatever it takes, to get whatever you want, however you want it.

Success for many is deemed by how many followers you have, likes you have, and subscribers you have. But being popular doesn't mean you are profitable.

We know the world's way:

No integrity? No problem.

Use God's name to claim success but ignore what He says? No problem.

Show everyone how happy you are in a picture, but behind the scenes your life is crumbling? No problem.

When you see those around you climb the ranks, it's easy to feel frustrated, lose patience, and have an urge to rush the race He laid out for you up a notch. People may recognize you by the top 2% they do see, but what about the other

98% that they don't see?

That 98% is the legacy you are leaving. Not the 2%.

The 98% is:

How you love your husband
How you love your children
How you love your friends and family
How you practice your faith and live it out daily
How you handle your feelings when no one but God sees
How you speak about others
How you provide excellent leadership and service to your customers in private messages

My friend, that 98% list is not something you can measure by likes, followers, and subscribers.

I was reading in Genesis 26 and these two words stopped me: "because Abraham." In Genesis 26:1-5, God is talking to Isaac about his promises. God's promises to Isaac were fulfilled because Abraham (his father) obeyed God's voice and kept His charge, commandments, statutes, and laws.

One man's obedience changed future generations.

Whether you have children or not, you are still leaving a legacy behind you.

The way you live, work, act, and feel behind closed doors and not in front of the masses is a part of your legacy.

Your climb to the 2% isn't bad. Unless it is.

Your success isn't bad. Unless it is.

It's the things we do that no one sees that make the greatest impact in the Kingdom.

What legacy are you leaving behind?

"Because (insert your name)..."

Father, remind our hearts that our race with You is way more important than the chase for anything else. Show us or strip us of anything that we can't see that isn't serving You so that we can leave a legacy that points people to You. We are willing and able. We love You! Amen!

59

HE KNOWS YOU BY NAME

. . . .

"The watchman opens the gate for him, and the sheep listen to his voice. He calls his own sheep by name and leads them out."

John 10:3

Liz Patton

Last week we attended a ceremony at my [Liz] youngest son's school. It was a pretty big deal to him because in years past, he sat through this very same ceremony for both of his older brothers. It was finally his turn. He had earned his time to shine.

The students were all lined up alphabetically, and I could see him excitedly waiting to hear his name so that he could walk across the stage. Except, when it was his turn, the teacher accidentally called him by his older brother's name instead. *[Womp-womp.]*

His teacher immediately recognized what she did and corrected herself, and he happily walked across to get his certificate. We all made a joke out of it because the truth is, we could all relate! Chances are you've messed up someone's name before too – either by forgetting their name or calling them by the wrong name, right?

But the next morning during my quiet time, I found myself reading the story of "The Shepherd and His Flock" in John 10:1-18 with new eyes. *(I'd love for you to read these verses for yourself and then come back so we can dive in together!)*

I especially love John 10:3: ***"The watchman opens the gate for him, and the sheep listen to his voice. He calls his own sheep by name and leads them out."***

I did some research into this whole watchman, shepherd, and sheep situation and learned that the sheep were kept in a large fenced area where they would spend the night. This "sheepfold" didn't provide protection for just one flock belonging to one shepherd—there were several flocks belonging to different shepherds. When the shepherds came to call their sheep to themselves "by name", the sheep would know the voice of their shepherd and follow their own shepherd only.

Does this give you goosebumps too?! Sister, if you're feeling forgotten, unseen, unworthy, or insignificant today, I pray this brings you comfort and hope. Not only does your good, good Father see you, but He knows you by name, and He is calling you to Himself.

Let's keep reading in verse 4, *"When he has brought out all his own, he goes on ahead of them, and his sheep follow him because they know his voice. But they will never follow a stranger; in fact, they will run away from him because they do not recognize a stranger's voice."*

Not only does your Good Shepherd call you by name, but once He has your attention, He wants to go ahead of you and lead you to where He wants you to go. For those of you who may be control freaks, or for those of you who may be feeling aimless today, I hope this encourages you. You don't have to have it all figured out. You don't have to be the one in control. All you have to do is listen for your Shepherd's voice and follow where He leads.

But here's the thing…we don't know what our Shepherd's voice sounds like if we aren't spending time with Him. In fact, according to verse 4, we might even follow a stranger's voice if we aren't spending enough time with our Shepherd in order to recognize His voice. THAT will preach!

Let's face it—in this crazy busy world that we live in, there are lots of voices competing for our attention. Lots. Our husbands, children, schedules, social media, volunteer and ministry opportunities, success, commitments, etc. Today, let's purpose in our hearts to spend more time listening for our Good Shepherd's voice and less time listening to the world. Let's let His voice be louder than any others! Because when we do that, He will give us life and life to the full!

Dear God, oh how I love being Yours! Thank You that You know me by name. Thank You that You lead me. Forgive me for the times I've been too busy or distracted to hear Your voice. I desire and purpose in my heart to hear and know Your voice above all others. You are my Good Shepherd, and I will follow You wherever You go. I love You. Amen.

60

DEALING WITH DOUBT

. . . .

"You're not a total failure if you doubt. You just can't stay there."

Michelle Myers

John the Baptist has always been one of the people in the Bible that has fascinated me [Michelle] the most. I mean, he wore clothes made of camel hair with a leather belt. He ate bugs and wild honey.

I have this "mountain man for Jesus" picture in my head. A guy who prepared the way for Jesus' ministry with boldness and passion. A man so godly, that he was chosen to baptize Jesus Himself.

And I'm not sure why I've always brushed past it, but it wasn't until reading carefully this year that John stopped being this "perfect Bible hero" in my brain and he became human.

Jesus' baptism was the beginning of Jesus' public ministry. He began teaching, performing miracles, and continuing the message John had been sharing. But at some point after baptizing Jesus, John was thrown into prison.

Look closely at Matthew 11:2-3:

"Now when John, while imprisoned, heard of the works of Christ, he sent word by his disciples and said to Him, "Are You the Expected One, or shall we look for someone else?"

John.

John the Baptist.

Jesus-mountain-man, bug-eating, leather-wearing, Jesus-baptizing JOHN...doubted.

Now before you change your mind about this true hero of the faith, put yourself in his shoes. He spent his adult life telling everyone that Jesus was coming, urging them to repent.

Then, Jesus comes on the scene.

At first, everything is great. John gets to baptize Jesus. He even realizes that, now that Jesus is here, it's his role to fade into the background (John 3:30).

But then, Herod throws John into prison. And now, as he's waiting to die, John begins to hear of what Jesus is doing…but it doesn't look like what John expected. John thought judgment was supposed to fall on those who would not repent and blessing would follow those who would believe.

We have no way of dissecting John's thoughts this side of Heaven, but I can only imagine that, if it were me, I would be thinking, "I thought my role in all of this would be different. I always expected to be less than you, Jesus, but I'll be honest: I expected to be there with You."

Maybe you can relate to some of those feelings.

But, as we say often here, feelings generally don't make a wise compass.

Look at Jesus' response:

"Jesus answered and said to them, "Go and report to John what you hear and see: the blind receive sight and the lame walk, the lepers are cleansed and the deaf hear, the dead are raised up and the poor have the gospel preached to them. And blessed is he who does not take offense at Me." (Matthew 11:4-6).

You're not a total failure if you doubt. You just can't stay there.

When we find ourselves doubting, we have to look at the evidence of what God is doing, not just in our current circumstance, but what He's done in the world throughout time.

When we doubt, the easy choice is to turn away. But if we choose to turn toward Him, it won't take long for the facts of who He is to take over our feelings.

So the next time you doubt, remind yourself of all the ways He's worked in the past. Use God's past faithfulness to interpret your current circumstance.

God, You are so faithful. Forgive us when we doubt You, but thank You for being quick to forgive us. Remind us often of Your past faithfulness. Help us to be disciplined in gratitude to remember the many blessings we have because of You. Increase our faith, Lord. We love You and we trust You. Amen.

61

EVEN IF

. . . .

"People > Position"

Emily Copeland

To my fellow introverts and extroverts: If you prefer to remain behind the scenes, regardless of your efforts, you will always have influence (no lack of eye contact or sitting quietly in conversation can get you out of it). If you are a woman who loves to live life out loud, you especially cannot escape your influence (the spotlight is great for revealing both talents and blemishes). To state the obvious, influence results in making an impact which can be both positive and negative. Since we are women who want to bring glory to the Kingdom, I [Emily] want to show you just how important your seat of choice is in the Kingdom of God today.

"When Peter came to Antioch, I [Paul] opposed him to his face, because he stood condemned. For before certain men came from James, he used to eat with the Gentiles. But when they arrived, he began to draw back and separate himself from the Gentiles because he was afraid of those who belonged to the circumcision group. The other Jews joined him in his hypocrisy, so that by their hypocrisy even Barnabas was led astray." Galatians 2:11-13.

Yes, you're reading this right. Paul opposed Peter to his face in front of a large crowd of important people. This is the same Peter who was radically changed forever by the resurrection and fully committed to sharing the gospel with the Gentiles. This is the same Peter who would later die for his faith. Even though he knew better (remember his denial of Jesus three times?), Peter shrunk back in fear. And Paul just about blew a gasket.

Peter was so concerned about the prominent Jewish leaders who were invited to this function that he abandoned the Gentiles and refused to sit with them. In other words, Peter began living by the law again. Rules > people. Position > people. How could this happen? How could he abort his mission so quickly?

Without a doubt, Peter knew that he held influence with the Jews and Gentiles. But, his choice to abandon his mission in the moment ultimately came out of a severely unhealthy perspective.

1. Peter impulsively responded with pride instead of humility. **"For before certain men came from James, he used to eat with the Gentiles." (v. 12)**

2. Peter reacted in his flesh which opened his heart to the fear of men. **"But when they arrived, he began to draw back and separate himself from the Gentiles because he was afraid of those who belonged to the circumcision group." (v.12)**

3. Peter experienced forgetfulness of the heart of the Gospel. **"I have been crucified with Christ and I no longer live, but Christ lives in me. The life I now live in the body, I live by faith in the Son of God, who loved me and gave Himself for me." (v.20)**

I say this often: If you are reading this devotion, you are a woman of influence. And as a human being, you and I are prone to wander when the pressure is on. With influence in our work and at home, our impact is determined by God alone in His response to our obedience. Will we get our hands dirty serving the mission? Or will we wipe our hands clean and sit in the comfortable seats away from those who need Jesus?

"I do not set aside the grace of God, for if righteousness could be gained through the law, Christ died for nothing!" (v. 21)

We must keep our hands in kingdom work so that our ego never grows beyond serving His people.

People > Performance
People > Position
People > Prestige
People > Privilege
People > Perception
People > Platform

Our automatic favor with God as His daughters and Kingdom ambassadors does not automatically mean that we have favor with all people. Peter experienced backlash when he tried to make the wrong people happy. Paul was quick to point out that Peter's influence would have a severely negative impact if he continued to choose pride, fear of man, and forgetfulness of the gospel each time the opportunity arose.

Ladies, it's more important for us to have an impact in a smaller way by doing the right thing than to have a great impact while ignoring the people that God has placed in our path. Your work will have a legacy. The world will tell you to choose the path that makes you look most worthy. God says to choose the path that makes others look better than yourself and the path that brings God the most glory.

He has called us to serve people, not a platform. Will you choose to sit with and serve those who can make your name famous? Or will you choose to sit with and serve those to whom God has given you influence in the Kingdom?

God, thank You for giving us an influence that doesn't just make people feel good, but an influence that can introduce them to You for the first time. Draw us in and give us the courage to see the people who need You most. May we point all eyes to You as we walk across the room, leaving our pride, fear, and forgetfulness behind to sit in the seat that You've called us to today. We love You. Amen.

62

YOU ARE SENT

. . . .

"The very reason you want to leave where God has you may be the very reason He has you there."

Michelle Myers

"I don't want to go home!" I [Michelle] pleaded. "Can't we just stay here?"

I was in the sixth grade, and it was time to leave church camp. We'd had an incredible week of worship and Bible teaching. And for a brief moment in time, the cliques that formed with our school social groups had disappeared. I felt known. I felt accepted. I felt safe.

But I knew that once we got in the buses to head back to our church, it wouldn't take long for things to go back to "normal."

You know what I mean by normal. Peer pressure. Temptation. Distraction. Discouragement. Division.

I've had several different moments in life where I've wanted to retreat for good since that one church camp. I mean, how appealing does it sound to live in a world free of those things?!

But listen to the words from Jesus' prayer the night of His betrayal:

"I do not ask You to take them out of the world, but to keep them from the evil one." John 17:15

Let that sink in:

Jesus did not ask God to help us withdraw from the world.

We live in a hurting, broken world. And while we may want nothing to do with it, Jesus is the only Solution to solve it. We have been entrusted with His message and to continue His work, so we must not look for opportunities to make our lives

139

more comfortable. We must tirelessly serve to ensure others' eternal comfort.

And tirelessly serving is uncomfortable. Somer Phoebus would say "beyond uncomfortable," it will probably often feel "none-comfortable."

In fact, just a few verses later, in vs. 18, Jesus says that He is sending us into the world, just as God sent Him into the world.

Think about that: The same authority that brought Jesus down to earth *sends you* to minister to a world that is desperate for the hope of salvation.

And despite the difficulty, we are to use our influence for good, without being influenced by evil.

Jesus has sent us into the world, but He prayed that we wouldn't fall for the enemy's tricks. That we wouldn't get self-absorbed, enslaved to sin, or stuck on secondary issues.

It's not easy, but He doesn't ask us to do it alone. God always goes before us. It's just up to us to make sure we're following Him and not the crowd.

I don't know where God has called you. Maybe you're in a job where talking about your faith is forbidden. You constantly feel like you're all alone, and sometimes, you just wish He would let you leave and do something else.

The very reason you want to leave where God has you may be the very reason He has you there. He asks us to shine our light in the darkness.

Never forget that you arrive nowhere by accident. You've been sent by God and for God. And He's with you every step of the way.

God, thank You for who You are and that You never ask us to go anywhere without Your presence. God, help us to realize that we are where we are, not by accident, but by an intentional Father, who loves each of His children, even the ones who are not walking with Him. Break our hearts for the world around us. Use us, and give us opportunities to shine Your light on those around us. Give us strength when we want to retreat, and protect us from the lies this world will offer us at every turn. Guard us in Your truth. We love You. Amen.

63

WHEN YOU FEEL LESS THAN

. . . .

"How much time do we spend valuing what others are doing
and devaluing what He is calling us to do?"

Jessica Hottle

**"Whoever says he is in the light and hates his brother is still in darkness.
Whoever loves his brother abides in the light, and in him there is no cause for
stumbling. But, whoever hates his brother is in the darkness and walks in the
darkness, and does not know where he is going, because the darkness has
blinded his eyes." 1 John 2:9-11**

As I [Jessica] read the Scripture above, my heart goes right to comparison,
because it happens so much amongst women. How much time do we spend
valuing what others are doing and devaluing what He is calling us to do?

Comparing yourself to her and wishing you were her is still taking your eyes off of
who He made you to be.

When you idolize her, you no longer put God first. She becomes your idol and
hope of inspiration versus the One who gives you the inspiration.

So much time is being wasted wishing you had the gifts she has or wishing you
had favor like she does.

It's exhausting to wish. It leads us nowhere but into defeat.

John wrote, **"Whoever says he is in the light and hates his brother is still in
darkness." (v. 9)**

Although you may not hate your sister, isn't comparison and jealousy just as much
a sin as anything else? Sin is sin. There's no hierarchy or levels or degrees. In
God's eyes, sin is sin.

When we hate, we don't see Jesus.

When we compare, we don't see Jesus.

When we are jealous, we don't see Jesus.

We no longer worship Him but the person we compare ourselves to. Therefore, we have gone from light to darkness.

Verse 10 continues with, **"Whoever loves his brother abides in the light and in him there is no cause for stumbling."** Even though John may not be talking about jealousy or comparison here, the truth remains the same: When we walk alongside our sister in Christ to pursue Christ, neither one of us stumbles, because we are both women on mission running after the same goal.

Friend, you can't compare (or be jealous) and still be in the light. It's a truth-bomb and gut-check all at once that I, too, have needed.

Comparison has done more than steal your joy. It takes away the light. It causes you to stumble and it causes you to look at your sister as the enemy.

Do you have a heart that has been comparing lately? Remember this: The same light that is in her, is in you! When you start comparing, choose instead to pray for her, then thank God for what He has given you!

Father, today I want to pray for the woman next to me. Give her strength, courage, and perseverance to fight the battles before her that no one may know about but You. Give her the wisdom to make the right choices, the patience to see her prayers be answered, and the peace that reminds her no other woman is her competition or enemy. We love You. Amen!

64

THE SPICE GIRLS

. . . .

"Who will roll the stone away from the entrance of the tomb?"

Mark 16:3

Liz Patton

Have you ever been so passionate about serving or working for the Lord that you jumped right into a task without even having a clear, well-organized plan? And maybe the way you wanted to serve your Savior even seemed foolish to the rest of the world, but you did it anyway? If so, I [Liz] am getting ready to share a biblical example with you that's hopefully going to give you so much inspiration!

While I was reading the account in Mark 16 of the women who traveled early in the morning to anoint the body of Jesus after He was crucified, I was struck by a few details that filled my heart with so much hope for us *she works His way* women!

First of all, I love so much that the women already had planned ahead and purchased the spices that they would use to anoint Jesus in order to show their love and devotion to Him. Because no purchases were able to be made on the Sabbath, this means that they would have needed to purchase these spices either late Friday night or after 6 p.m. on Saturday evening. That's some determination right there. But their Savior was worth it!

Secondly, all four gospels suggest that the women left for the tomb of Jesus early in the morning: (Matthew 28:1, "*at dawn,*" Mark 16:1 and Luke 24:1, "*very early,*" and John 20:1 "*while it was still dark.*") These women were on a mission. Even though it was the disciples who spent the majority of their time with Jesus, it was these women who were thoughtful, committed, and caring enough to take this journey to attend to the body of Jesus. Go girls!!

This next example is what made my soul bubble up with hope and excitement – while the women were on their way to the tomb, they asked each other, **"Who will roll the stone away from the entrance of the tomb?" Mark 16:3**

Don't you just love it so much?! The thought hadn't even occurred to these Jesus-loving girls that they would need to figure out a way to roll away the stone in order to get inside to their Jesus! They just wanted to be obedient to serve Him and to show their love for Him, and so off they went! If they had shared their idea with the disciples or someone in their family, perhaps they might have been talked out of it. But there was no people-pleasing, perfection paralysis, or fear of judgment in these women! They just kept their eyes focused on being obedient to loving and serving their Jesus!

That's why I think it's so special that He blessed their obedience – when they got to the tomb, the stone had already been rolled away and the angel told them, **"Don't be alarmed. You are looking for Jesus the Nazarene, who was crucified. He has risen! He is not here. See the place where they laid him. But go, tell his disciples." Mark 16:6-7.** Because of their obedience, these women got the honor and privilege of sharing the Good News with the disciples!

What can we learn and take away from these dedicated women who were followers of Jesus?

1. Rise early! *Are we getting up before the rest of our family and/or work commitments to spend time with our Savior?*

2. Be prepared! They knew what spices they needed to anoint Jesus, and so they planned around their Sabbath to ensure they would be prepared. *Are we gathering the resources we need to be prepared to get our jobs done?* (Just a little side note—we have TONS of classes and resources available in our membership portal for women desiring to work God's way! If you're not a member yet, what are you waiting for?) ;)

3. Jump in! They didn't need to see the entire plan before taking the first step. They didn't fear judgment or ridicule; they didn't need to please anyone; and they also didn't need to know all the details before heading out for the tomb. They were focused on serving their Savior, and that's all that mattered. *Are we trying to people-please? Do we fear failure so much that our "perfection paralysis" keeps us stuck rather than jumping in to serve our Savior?*

4. God blessed their obedience! He showed Himself to them first. *Are we defining our success as obedience? Not worldly recognition, a bigger platform, more followers, or more income. Just obedience.*

Let's be like the original "Spice Girls," the women who were devoted to loving and serving Jesus with their whole hearts!

Dear God, we love You! We desire to rise early, be prepared, and jump in to serve You. Help us to realize that we don't have to know every single little detail before we can serve You – we just need to have our hearts and eyes set on You. Help us be brave enough to define our success as obedience alone. Thank You for dying for us and for the promise of eternal life with You. We love You. Amen.

65

FEAR

. . . .

"It's okay to feel fearful as long as you're still faithful!"

Somer Phoebus

It's okay to feel fearful as long as you're still faithful!

We talk about fear as a tool that the enemy can use to paralyze us, and it is! But what I [Somer] am learning is fear is also a very natural reaction to the things God is calling you to. For me, when God asks me to do something or go somewhere, it's not usually a mission that involves zero risk. Even in something as basic as sharing the gospel with someone, it's scary. I fear their reaction, I fear how well I'll deliver the message, and I fear that they will ultimately reject it.

Fear is a real thing and it happens to even mature believers.

Can you imagine how Peter felt when he started to sink after God called him out of the boat to walk on water? **(Matthew 14)**

Can you imagine how Gideon felt when God dwindled his army down to 300 only to fight a much larger army? **(Judges 7)**

Can you imagine how Mary felt when the Angel of the Lord told her she would give birth to Jesus? **(Luke 1)**

Fear is a part of our walk with Christ, because in a lot of instances, fear is an appropriate response. Fearing something doesn't mean you lack faith unless your fear stops you from doing that thing.

One of the questions/comments I hear so often is, "How do I get past my fear? I'm praying that God will deliver me from it so I can do what He's called me to, but it's not working!"

The answer that I've discovered and now get to give is that sometimes we don't get past it.

145

SHE WORKS HIS WAY

We don't get past it because sometimes God is asking us to do it afraid!

I just wonder what would happen if, instead of focusing so much on the fear, we focused on the mission. What if we decided to be thankful for the fear because we realized it's the means to a deeper faith? How many of us are in a holding pattern because we're trying to pray away the fear before we take a step forward, when God is asking us to step out in the midst of our fear despite it?

Maybe we're telling ourselves that what He's calling us to can't be the right thing because, if it were the right thing, we wouldn't feel fearful. Be very careful making assumptions like that. Fear doesn't always mean the absence of peace and peace doesn't always mean the absence of fear. I personally have often been fearful of what's next but at complete peace as I walked right into it. Mary was my example of this. Fearful for sure. But also at peace because she knew she was being used by God and that He would ultimately take care of her!

And Mary said, *"Behold, I am the servant of the Lord; let it be to me according to your word." And the angel departed from her. Luke 1:38*

It's okay to feel fearful as long as you're faithful!

Will you walk in faith even when you fear what's ahead?

Will you do it afraid?

God, I pray that You would let nothing stop me from what it is You are calling me to. I pray that my fear would only increase my faith. God show me how to move forward even when I'm fearful and use me in spite of that fear. I pray that You will get the glory as I go about Your work today and every day! Amen.

66

PERSISTENT PRAYER

. . . .

"Your 'behind the scenes' is way more important
than any 'highlight reel.'"

Jessica Hottle

"God, did I do something wrong?" I [Jessica] asked.

"Did I not hear Your voice?" I continued.

"Did I not pray enough or pray the right thing?" I questioned.

Sometimes, if I am being honest, those questions are real questions I ask the Lord when things begin not to go the way that I would like them to go, when things don't seem or feel like they are getting better. Maybe you can relate too?

When you feel the weight of what feels like a wilderness season, it's easy to think that your prayers must have not been heard.

...But God.

God speaks to you when you feel like you are in the wilderness, wandering around, trying to find your way to the Promised Land.

I've realized that ministry work – God's work – is never in one location, one thing. It never looks like you thought it would be, and, the more you mature in Christ, the more He wrecks your heart.

So, if you are feeling all the feels, the uncomfortable stretch, you are usually in the right spot. Can I just say that I'm there with you?! Feeling all the feels, the pull, and the stretch.

Don't allow this to be a time where you pull away because nothing seems to make sense. Let this be a time where you press in and feel those feels.

The widow in Jesus's parable in Luke 18:1-8 brings hope to my soul:

Then Jesus told his disciples a parable to show them that they should always pray and not give up. He said: "In a certain town there was a judge who neither feared God nor cared what people thought. And there was a widow in that town who kept coming to him with the plea, 'Grant me justice against my adversary.'

For some time, he refused. But finally, he said to himself, 'Even though I don't fear God or care what people think, yet because this widow keeps bothering me, I will see that she gets justice, so that she won't eventually come and attack me!'"

And the Lord said, "Listen to what the unjust judge says. And will not God bring about justice for his chosen ones, who cry out to him day and night? Will he keep putting them off? I tell you, he will see that they get justice, and quickly. However, when the Son of Man comes, will he find faith on the earth?"

This parable tells us that persistent prayers are Kingdom-focused. Therefore, the instant gratifications many of us want often come from a different kingdom.

It reminds us that He does hear us and that, in His time, our prayers will be answered. Persistence and perseverance are our choice. As *she works His way* women, they should be our top choices over quick, easy, and fast.

Let me encourage your heart, my friend, that even though you may not see fruit in the natural world, He's doing the work in the supernatural world. Your "behind the scenes" is way more important than any "highlight reel."

God is after your heart. How are you surrendering it to Him in the season you are in?

Father, thank You for answering my prayers in Your way and in Your time. Allow patience to persevere and rule over fear and worry in my life. Anything that is weighing me down – please bring it to my attention. Speak to me in a way that I know could only be You. I love You. In Jesus name, Amen!

67

IMPOSSIBLE = OPPORTUNITY

. . . .

"A task that is impossible for you becomes an opportunity for others to see God."

Michelle Myers

We talk often around here about how the business world gets us accustomed to measurables and metrics. There's something oddly comfortable about numbers and facts that allow us to see results.

And while there's nothing necessarily wrong in itself with having those metrics, if we allow ourselves to get too wrapped up in what is logical, practical, and doable, we can sometimes miss a huge, unpredictable element in working God's way:

God.

Let's look at Mark 6 for an example of how the disciples reacted when they were given an "impossible" task:

"By this time it was late in the day, so his disciples came to Him. "This is a remote place," they said, "and it's already very late. Send the people away so that they can go to the surrounding countryside and villages and buy themselves something to eat." But He answered, "You give them something to eat." They said to Him, "That would take more than half a year's wages! Are we to go and spend that much on bread and give it to them to eat?" "How many loaves do you have?" He asked. "Go and see." When they found out, they said, "Five—and two fish." Mark 6:35-38

Now, most of us can admit that we probably would have reacted the same way the disciples did to Jesus' words. Coming up with food for 5,000 people is no easy feat.

But the disciples didn't get it. Somehow, even though Jesus was right there in front of them and they had witnessed Him perform many miracles, they still had it in their heads that they were bound by their own limits.

Our work may be bound by our limits, but God's work is limitless.

Let's notice what Jesus did. He didn't just snap his fingers and make food appear.

"Taking the five loaves and the two fish and looking up to heaven, He gave thanks and broke the loaves. Then he gave them to his disciples to distribute to the people. He also divided the two fish among them all. They all ate and were satisfied." Mark 6:41-42

Jesus involves us. He asked the disciples to go and see what food they could gather. Then, He took the food they found and multiplied it into more.

He expects us to do what we can, but we get to depend on Him for the rest.

So, let's do some honest evaluation:

How do you react when given an impossible task?

Do you see what you have, do what you can, pray for God's blessings, and expect Him to work?

Or do you examine it according to your own limits, decide the predictable outcome on your own, and miss an opportunity for God to make the impossible possible?

God is the most important element in doing God's work. If we claim to do God's work, but leave no room for Him to do His part, we are only fooling ourselves.

Doing God's work means He will often call us beyond our own limits so others get to see Him. Because if He is the point of the work, people have to be able to see beyond us for God to get the glory.

So as you do His work, remember this always:

A task that is impossible for you becomes an opportunity for others to see God.

Let's do what we can and trust Him for the rest.

God, we confess that it's so easy to make Your work about us. Our limits. What we can do. Outcomes we can predict. But we know that nothing is impossible with You. We know that You will often call us beyond what we feel we are capable of doing. But God, we also know that You are faithful to complete what You start. God, increase our faith and remind us of Your purposes when we are given tasks that feel impossible. We trust You and we love You. Amen.

68

TO KNOW

. . . .

"Carrying the knowledge of truth is not just a privilege,
it's our greatest responsibility."

Emily Copeland

Having knowledge and understanding is the best place to start, but it should never be the final destination.

If you had the cure for cancer, but never shared it, you'd be withholding incredibly valuable information, right?

If you knew that your daughter was being bullied at school, but never talked to her about it, you'd be holding back love.

We can't imagine the thought of remaining silent in either of these situations. We wouldn't just be grateful for the knowledge, we would recognize that it is our responsibility and duty to step into what's broken and share our knowledge.

But how often do we subdue our God-assigned gifts and responsibility of using them out of fear?

In Luke 12:47-48 we see two servants who have been put in charge of their master's possessions while he is gone. One faithfully waits and serves in obedience to his master while another grows impatient and begins following his own plan and desires.

"The servant who knows the master's will and does not get ready or does not do what the master wants will be beaten with many blows. But the one who does not know and does things deserving punishment will be beaten with few blows. From everyone who has been given much, much will be demanded; and from the one who has been entrusted with much, much more will be asked."

There are two human responses to knowledge and responsibility: to know and to hold back, and to know and to take action.

What has God called you to do? How has He gifted you differently than other women? Are you using your talents for God or holding them back?

Let me [Emily] boldly remind you: As a daughter of God, you've been gifted in talent and knowledge of the truth. You've also been given responsibility to use your talent and knowledge without holding back. Friends, holding back is disobedience. Holding back is a serious offense to the Kingdom. It may feel safer to remain quiet and to fly under the radar, but it is actually quite the opposite.

It's possible to create earthly success in business or in achievements that ultimately don't require much of the talents or gifts that God has given you that point people back to Him. This is more dangerous than the person who is unable to share because they don't have knowledge (vs. 48).

Having the responsibility of knowing truth and carrying gifts to connect people to the truth is the privilege of a lifetime! If you've allowed the world to condition you into silence or into believing that your responsibility as a Christ-follower is minimal, then it's time for a do-over. His grace is abundant and overflowing!

Will you pray with me?

God, putting Jesus on the cross set us free and gave us the privilege to use our one life to point it all back to You. We hold knowledge of the truth and we carry the responsibility to use what You've given us and to not hold back. Make us aware today of the gifts and talents that we have held back from You. Help us to see where the world has de-sensitized our hearts and minds towards the mission. We've been entrusted with so much. Thank You for including us in Your plan. We love You! Amen.

69

LIFE IS BUT A WEAVING

. . . .

*"Although the threads of my life have often
seemed knotted, I know, by faith, that on the other
side of the embroidery there is a crown."*
- Corrie ten Boom

Liz Patton

My mom is super crafty. She used to sew the clothes that my brother and I [Liz] wore growing up. She makes all of her own wreaths and decorations in her home, and she even did the flowers for my wedding. I, on the other hand, am lucky if I can sew a button on my boys' shirts and am downright dangerous with a glue gun. I most certainly did not inherit her crafty gene.

As a small girl, I asked her to teach me how to make cross-stitch gifts for my friends at Christmastime. What I remember most is that the underside of the fabric was a total mess, but surprisingly, when I turned it over, it actually came together as a beautiful gift.

Imagine my delight when I was reading about Corrie ten Boom (a brave, Dutch Christian who helped many Jews escape Nazi persecution during World War II) who would use this embroidery illustration when she was asked to speak about her experience. When talking to people about the importance of trusting in God's plan for their lives, she would show them a piece of cloth with a jumble of colored threads that seemed to be a tangled, chaotic mess. She would then read this poem by Grant Colfax Tullar:

Life is But a Weaving

*My life is but a weaving
Between my God and me.
I cannot choose the colors
He weaveth steadily.
Oft' times He weaveth sorrow;*

And I in foolish pride
Forget He sees the upper
And I the underside.
Not 'til the loom is silent
And the shuttles cease to fly
Will God unroll the canvas
And reveal the reason why.
The dark threads are as needful
In the weaver's skillful hand
As the threads of gold and silver
In the pattern He has planned
He knows, He loves, He cares;
Nothing this truth can dim.
He gives the very best to those
Who leave the choice to Him.

What I love most about Corrie ten Boom's illustration is that she would then turn the cloth over, revealing what the weaving really was—A beautiful crown! She would say: "Although the threads of my life have often seemed knotted, I know, by faith, that on the other side of the embroidery there is a crown."

It's so easy for us to focus on the messy chaos in our lives because we aren't looking at the big picture! We have a tendency to look at the confused and tangled underside. When that is our focus, we miss out on the peace and joy that comes from walking closely with our Master Weaver.

When we remember that God is in control, and that this current chaos is just a small piece of His master plan, we are able to get a glimpse of the beautiful upper side and trust in God's perspective. We can't see what He sees, but we can trust in His promise:

"The Lord will fulfill his purpose for me; your steadfast love, O Lord, endures forever. Do not forsake the work of your hands." Psalm 138:8

Dear God, I am so grateful that You are the One in control of my life, and not me. When I can't see the big picture or when I'm focused on the messy chaos of my life, I find comfort in knowing that Your steadfast love endures forever. You are looking at the beautiful embroidery on the other side, and for that I am forever grateful. I trust You and I love You. Amen.

70

THE ANSWER

. . . .

"When we make it about us, we cease to worship Him."

Somer Phoebus

I [Somer] am discovering that there is a very simple answer to a chronic complaint that has plagued almost all believers I've spent time with lately. Keep in mind, a lot of my ministry time is spent with teenagers through college students, and let me tell ya, our society has trained them well to consider themselves above all else, that self-care and their own ideals and feelings are more important than most other things in life.

Before I go on, I want to make sure you understand I am not anti self-care, nor do I think it is healthy to ignore our thoughts and feelings or to keep them to ourselves. However, I do believe as with so many things in our world, that in an effort to make humans better, we've made God smaller and ourselves larger. Basically, we're formulating a plan that will encourage nominal Christianity and discourage all-in, surrendered Christ-followers.

So that chronic complaint with the simple answer I'm hearing so often is this...

"Why do I feel..." and then fill in the blank with your answer. The blank can be filled in with a multitude of things specific to the individual, but if the complaint begins the same every time, the answer is also the same every time.

Why do I feel...

Unhappy
Insignificant
Unsuccessful
Ignored
Depressed
Anxious
Left Out

The answer?

MISPLACED FOCUS.

Every. Time.

We're too busy looking in our mirror instead of looking to our Master.

Hear me when I say though, this does not mean that if your eyes are on God you won't experience any of those things above *(or whatever your own fill-in-the-blank answer is.)* Walking with God isn't easy. I know a lot of mature believers that struggle with anxiety, but one friend in particular reminded me that this hard place where she is walking is for HIS purpose, so she's okay! I believe she even used the word "honored" when she was talking about being used by God in this way.

You see, when we're focused on Jesus, we don't care about our symptoms as much as we do the purpose behind them. If God has you walking through a dark place like my friend, it's for a reason. Our job is to stay focused on HIS light.

Paul spent many of his days in prison, but he didn't ask "why me?" Instead, he thanked God for the opportunity to be used for His glory and he worshipped. **(See Acts 16:16-40)**

Here's a question I've been asking myself and those I am discipling as well: How many times a day do we use the word "I" or "me?" And how often is it in the midst of a sentence where the goal is to complain?

The more we complain, the more we're unhappy, and the more we're unhappy, the more we complain.

But if we truly understood what Jesus did for us and what we've been delivered from, we would laugh at even the thought that something isn't fair or that our life is too hard. We wouldn't dare be irritable over our situation that isn't ideal or is not what we had hoped for.

The bottom line is that we were not made to worry about ourselves, because we were not made for the sake of ourselves. It's extremely unnatural to our spiritual selves – our new man in Christ (2 Cor 5:17) – to focus on our own feelings and emotions. So if you're noticing a constant tension that you're calling unhappiness or discontentment you may want to check the cause of that uncomfortableness.

Could it be that you are fighting against your spiritual self by making yourself the center of your concern when the center of everything we are and everything we live for should be God?

When we make it about us, we cease to worship Him.

We have been created to do nothing but lift up and glorify God. That is our very purpose. Our ONLY purpose. Will you make Him the focus?

Dear God, please be the focus of my life and my worship. Lord, forgive me for being concerned with myself and for taking my eyes off of You. I ask You to reveal Yourself to me so that even in the midst of hard times I can see Your power at work within me and I can display Your glory for others to see. Thank You for loving me! I love You! Amen.

71

VULNERABLE

. . . .

"We must learn what God's voice sounds like through His word
and refuse to follow unless it's His voice that we hear."

Emily Copeland

If you enjoy a good formal devotion without any vulnerability, this may not be a good read for you today. (Also, if you don't giggle even just a little at my expense, you may need to re-read it!)

Let me [Emily] just get right down to the point. Three weeks ago I had temporary teeth put in place of my top front four teeth. All of my life, my adult teeth have been too narrow, so I've always had my teeth shaped by cement (bonding). We knew the time would come when I would have to have veneers, and this month happened to be that time. Little did I know that I would spend most of the month with temporary teeth that could fall out at any time. Constant panic has been my companion. Toothless visions have haunted me day and night. How's that for vulnerable?

This also happened to be one of the busiest and most exciting months of my entire life. It included travel, new leadership opportunities, social gatherings and best of all, the birth of my precious new little nephew, Holland Thomas. All while wondering if I would be fully exposed if I chomped down too hard while eating or speaking in front of all of the women at the MOPS event I spoke at.

Friends, life doesn't stop for anything. You may feel more vulnerable now than ever before. Maybe you've started a new business or invested heavily into a dream that God has given you.

When we are most vulnerable, we are also most open to people's opinions and most burdened by people's expectations of us. When we've put ourselves out there, we simultaneously tend to put on a radar that picks up on everyone's thoughts and opinions. Their voices grow louder and it becomes very easy for us to put a lot of stock into their opinions.

I want to remind you of one great big truth today: God's voice is the only one that matters.

How do we know?

God has desired to be the only voice since the very beginning;

"And the Lord God commanded the man, "You are free to eat from any tree in the garden; but you must not eat from the tree of the knowledge of good and evil, for when you eat of it you will surely die." Genesis 2:16-17

Voice #2 (Satan) steps in; **"You will not certainly die." Genesis 3:4**

God didn't command Adam just for kicks and giggles. He spoke with Adam in order to keep the peace, continue to live in harmony, and to receive the glory.

Your vulnerability is God's opportunity to shape you unless you let the world's voice become a megaphone into your situation.

How do we listen to God's voice alone when the world can be so loud? We learn what His voice sounds like through His Word and, like sheep, we refuse to follow unless it's His voice that we hear.

"When he has brought out all his own, he goes on ahead of them, and his sheep follow Him because they know His voice." John 10:4

Invite God into your vulnerability today. Get alone with Him and learn His voice through His Word and then push away all other voices. Every call from God must be protected – Let's follow the Good Shepherd all the way.

God, thank You for using us. Thank You for making Your truths evident and clear in Your Word. You never hide Yourself from us. Help us to step forward courageously today in what we know You have called us to do. We love You! Amen.

72

STOP RUNNING

. . . .

*"Stop expecting something bad to happen in your business
and/or life because it could. Expect something good
to happen because it can. Because He can."*

Jessica Hottle

"I can't keep expecting something bad to happen because it could. I need to expect something good to happen because it can." I [Jessica] wrote this in my journal.

Prior to writing the sentences above I had just wrapped up reading Numbers 11.

In chapter 11, we see the Israelites complaining...again. They were weeping over misfortunes and the fact that they were hungry and wanted meat. Their most common thing to say was, "Why did we come out of Egypt?" As in: Why are we in the wilderness, in the unknown, walking all these miles, living this way with uncertainty of food and being tired until we get to this Promised Land, when we could simply be enslaved but have some kind of comfort?

Isn't this where we can sometimes find ourselves getting comfortable today? Enslaved by work but comforted by the results we may get no matter the cost of our walk with the Lord?

The Lord led them out of captivity to lead them through to wilderness to bless them in the Promised Land.

Before we judge the Israelites for complaining yet again, I think we can find ourselves in their story today.

They left a land they were familiar with. Although enslaved, they remembered **"the fish they ate in Egypt that cost nothing, the cucumbers, the melons, the leeks, the onions, and the garlic." (v. 5)** Something that was guaranteed, with minimal faith required.

Now they are being led through the wilderness (faith required!) by an ark and some clouds. At times, their food has been given to them just enough for a day and at a time and other times (like this one) the Lord gives them more than enough and gives them so much at once that **"it came out of their nostrils and became loathsome to it." (v. 20)**

The land of familiarity (the past) often hinders us from going into the land of possibility (the future).

Isn't the wilderness important for our growth, strength, courage, and faith? But, how often do we run from the growth the Lord is trying to lead us through to get to our Promised Land?

Let me encourage your heart today sister, STOP RUNNING.

Stop running to your past.
Stop running from the future.
Stop running from the wilderness.
Stop running, because your Promised Land awaits.

Stop expecting something bad to happen in your business and/or life because it could. Expect something good to happen because it can. Because He can.

Stop settling for mediocre comfort when you can bathe in a land that overflows with milk and honey.

Father, we are so grateful that You have a love that is tough and tender, a heart that is full of grace and mercy. When we want to run to our old ways, redirect and point us back to our future in You. Let us not be afraid of the unknown or the season that feels like the wilderness. Let us press in to be refined by You. We love You! Amen!

73

LITTLE = MUCH

. . . .

"People need what only you can give, so let God
work through you as a demonstration of His power."

Liz Patton

Do you ever go through seasons when you feel like you just stink at all the things?
Like you don't measure up or aren't enough? If so, you're not alone, my sweet
sister. In fact, I [Liz] was thinking about this recently while our family was at the
beach. I was noticing lots of people getting excited about finding and gathering
up the biggest sea shells on the beach, while I, on the other hand, was drawn to
the teeny, tiny shells.

I marveled at how perfect some of them were as they fit on the tip of my pinky
finger, even though they paled in comparison to the bigger shells. And this got
me thinking about my own recent feelings of inadequacy. I realized that I had
allowed the enemy to make me feel insufficient: insufficient to write this devotion
because I don't have a Bible degree, insufficient to lead a team because my
background is in education instead of business, insufficient to host a women's
Bible study in my home because I don't know enough, blah, blah, blah.

Not surprisingly, as God so often lovingly does, the next day I found this sweet
verse tucked in 1 Corinthians 2:4-5 (Paul is speaking here):

**"My message and my preaching were not with wise and persuasive words,
but with a demonstration of the Spirit's power, so that your faith might not
rest on men's wisdom, but on God's power."**

Oh my goodness! If the Apostle Paul felt insufficient and not wise or persuasive
enough, I guess I am in pretty good company! But I love Paul's reminder that it's
not about me or my wisdom, but rather God's power! Amen?!

We see this same theme in the Widow's Offering in Mark 12:41-44 when the rich
people were throwing in large amounts of money into the offering, and a poor
widow came and put in two very small coins, worth only a fraction of a penny.

162

And Jesus points out to his disciples, *"I tell you the truth, this poor widow has put more into the treasury than all the others. They all gave out of their wealth; but she, out of her poverty, put in everything—all she had to live on."*

What an encouragement this is to me! God sees what man overlooks. Surely the crowd, and maybe even the disciples, were noticing the big gifts (just like my fellow vacationers were noticing the big shells). But Jesus saw what no one else did *(the little coins...and for me the little shells)*, and it was the widow's gift that Jesus found worthy of comment. In fact, He said she put "more into the treasury than all the others."

Sisters, you have gifts that God has given to you that you can be using right this very minute. It's time to stop the feelings of unworthiness and put those gifts to good use! Stop comparing them to others' "bigger" gifts, and stop feeling like they're not grand enough or that you're not worthy enough. I want to encourage you today to go out and use the gifts God has given to you! People need what only you can give, so let God work through you as a demonstration of His power!

Dear God, thank You for the gifts You've given me. Forgive me for the times when I have compared them to others and for the times I haven't even recognized them for the gifts they truly are. Help me remember that it's not about my wisdom, but instead it's about Your power! Work through me, and give me the courage to go out and serve and love others in Your name and for Your glory. I love You. Amen.

74

LOVE VS. LUST

. . . .

"When it comes to your business, is there
more evidence of love or lust?"

Michelle Myers

*Just as a precaution before you read: If you have been a victim
of a sexual crime, this devo recounts the story of a rape from Scripture,
so it may contain trigger points for you.*

Reality TV has nothing on the Old Testament. If we want to find family dysfunction, drama, and scandal, all we need to do is open our Bibles.

And there may be no story more devastating than Amnon and Tamar, King David's son and daughter *(2 Samuel 13)*.

Short summary: Amnon became obsessed with his sister, Tamar, so much so that he actually made himself ill *(2 Samuel 13:2)*. His cousin, Jonadab, finally pried the truth out of him, and when Amnon claimed to be in love with Tamar, Jonadab helped him to devise a plan to rape her.

Tamar pleaded with Amnon not to violate her, but he was stronger than she was, so he was able to overpower her *(2 Samuel 13:12-14)*.

Immediately after he raped her, Scripture records that he was filled with intense hatred for her, and then sent her away, which Tamar claimed was an even greater offense than the rape *(2 Samuel 13:13-16)*.

Quickly, let's make some observations on the difference between love and lust:

Lust demands immediate satisfaction.

Love is patient *(1 Corinthians 13:4)*.

Lust deals harshly.

164

Love is kind *(1 Corinthians 13:4)*.

Lust dishonors others.

Love honors others *(1 Corinthians 13:5)*.

Lust demands its own way.

Love is not self-seeking *(1 Corinthians 13:5)*.

I [Michelle] doubt I need to spiritually break down how lust destroyed a family unit in this story. When incest and rape are involved, explanation is not really needed to dissect what went wrong.

But what does this teach us about lust in our own lives? Because lust is not limited to just sexual sin.

Lust can be defined as "a passionate or overmastering desire or craving."

So I'll just ask bluntly: **When it comes to your work, is there more evidence of love or lust?**

Do you have patience...or demand immediate satisfaction?

Are you kind...or do you deal harshly?

Do you honor others...or dishonor them?

Are you more likely to deny yourself...or demand your own way?

As we see in this story, lust destroys. Even if earthly success comes, what does it *ultimately* cost us if we are acting more out of lust than of love?

Because if we actually err more on the actions of lust, we don't really "love" our work, do we?

Today, let's ask God to really examine our hearts. Let's look at the traits that are so evident in Amnon and search ourselves for any similarities. Then, let's be intentional to remove any trace of lust from our lives that we may have disguised as love.

God, we love You. Thank You for being a God who can search us and know us. God, examine us today. Reveal any lingering trace of lust that exists in our hearts. Convict us, and help us to confess to You how we have fallen short. Then God, help us to correct our actions to display Your love in every area. Thank You for Your grace, Your forgiveness, and Your power to redeem. Amen.

75

SAFE AND SECURE

. . . .

"The pursuit of security is the opposite of surrender."

Somer Phoebus

In this crazy world, I [Somer] often hear so many parents say they just want to create a home where their children feel safe and secure. A bubble where they can hide their little family away and protect them from the sinfulness that is all around us. And that's not a bad thing – I get it. But my friend, it is FAR from the best thing.

Jonah ran away from surrender and toward security, which landed him in the belly of a large fish.

Lot's wife was not surrendered to God's plan and made the choice to look back at what she thought was security, which resulted in her instant transformation into a pile of salt.

All over Scripture, we see examples of God's people ignoring His direction for the sake of supposed safety and security. Never did it end well for them.

We see this, and yet we still struggle with it as well!

I was reading a book by Francis Chan where he mentioned the idea that believers have somehow decided that surrender can happen over time. But my friends, Jesus asked His disciples to quit everything, leave their lives behind, and follow Him IMMEDIATELY. He didn't ask them to start by giving a little more of their time every day. There wasn't a part time internship that they signed up for to make sure they were prepared to follow Him! There was just a commandment: "Follow Me."

"While walking by the Sea of Galilee, he saw two brothers, Simon (who is called Peter) and Andrew his brother, casting a net into the sea, for they were fishermen. And he said to them, "Follow me, and I will make you fishers of men." Immediately they left their nets and followed him. And going on from there he saw two other brothers, James the son of Zebedee and John

his brother, in the boat with Zebedee their father, mending their nets, and he called them. Immediately they left the boat and their father and followed him." Matthew 4:18-22

Listen, I really do want my kids to feel safe. But only because they trust Jesus.

I want my kids to feel stable. But only because they have experienced the peace that only Jesus could provide during very unstable times – the kind of joy in the midst of suffering that Paul speaks of!

I want my kids to feel secure. But only because they know that mom and dad are walking with Jesus, so wherever we go, He will take care of us.

You see, the pursuit of security is the opposite of surrender!

I think it's easy to talk about surrender because we've grown accustomed to believe that choosing to serve at church instead of heading to the Sunday morning brunch buffet with friends is surrender.

But surrender is not giving up a moment, or a thing. Surrender is the only reasonable response to what Jesus did for us on the cross. Surrender is the action we take in order to prove that we know we are not our own.

"Do you not know that your bodies are temples of the Holy Spirit, who is in you, whom you have received from God? You are not your own; you were bought at a price. Therefore honor God with your bodies." 1 Corinthians 6:19-20

Don't rob yourself or your family of the blessings *(and the incredible adventure)* that God will POUR out on you when you focus on living surrendered rather than "secure."

God, I want the life that You provide and nothing else! Help me to understand that in Your hands I am as safe as I can be. God, forgive me for the times that I have gotten in the way of You being able to use me or my family. Help me to have the faith to trust You no matter where it is that You take me. I love You! Amen.

76

NEW IN CHRIST

. . . .

"Before the business world ever gave you a title,
you were a daughter of the King first."

Jessica Hottle

Before you read today's devotional, head on over to Colossians 2:6-15 and read through the passage. Then meet me back here for discussion.

There are seven key points I [Jessica] want you to say and begin to speak in your life from the passage you read today. They are:

1. I am strong in spirit.
2. I am complete in Christ.
3. I have wisdom and discernment.
4. I have been set free from my past sin.
5. I am alive and forgiven.
6. I have been redeemed.
7. I have been given power and authority over the enemy.

We often hear things like, "In Christ, you have everything He has." Or, "Use what you have been given." But, I don't think many people realize WHAT they have been given. (I know I didn't for many years. And, He is still causing me to fully realize this in my life.)

You have been given spiritual power. You are reborn into a new body and union with Christ. You don't have to beg God for the things He has already given you. You simply need to understand what you have been given and then begin to live out these truths in your life. Here are some areas of life to consider how they might apply to you:

By the words you speak.

By the way you live your life.

By having only one God in your life.

By believing and understanding that He's not late on His promises for you.

By knowing that if it's not good, then it's not the end.

By understanding that He doesn't give bad reports, the enemy does.

By believing you are not weak, but strong.

No matter where your business is, we can look to His word and understand all that we have been given and know that, regardless of the results, regardless of the not-so-good outcome, regardless of the number of followers you have, you are still a daughter of the King and an heir to the crown.

That's your first title – Daughter – and it was your destiny before the business world ever tried to give you a title.

I have an assignment for you today.

From the seven key points above, I want you to ask yourself this question, "What's stopping me from living in this truth?"

The seven key points above are WHO you already are. It's our responsibility to unravel and break the walls we have built that are keeping us from fully stepping into it. And, when you step into who He made you to be, then your business changes, your marriage changes, and every area of your life changes.

So, journal it all. What lies have you believed?

Remember, the enemy is a master deceiver and a manipulator of God's Word. So, if you find yourself questioning the Truth, know it's probably the enemy trying to keep you from experiencing your union with Christ fully.

Father, open my heart today. Give me a new lens through which I view my life. Help me to see what You see and not what the enemy or the world wants me to see. Allow the tough questions to come up because I know they only make me stronger and set me free. I love You. In Your name, Amen!

77

GOD TO THE RESCUE

. . . .

"Because God can redeem it, let's declare it!"

Emily Copeland

We've all experienced it – a sunset so beautiful that we cannot take our eyes off of it. Each color is recognizable, but its full picture is nearly impossible to explain because you just have to see it to understand. Think about anything that has captivated you at first sight in this way. Now, has a portion of Scripture ever had this level of impact on you?

Whether your answer is yes or no, will you take just a couple of moments and read Psalm 107?

Unofficially titled, "God to the Rescue," this portion of Scripture shows the Redeemer of all creation stepping into four different types of distressed lives: Those who have been lost, those who have been found guilty, those who are sick, and those who have been tossed back and forth by life's storms. And, you guys, it's breathtaking.

There is an Israel Houghton song that is called "Say So," and the chorus simply repeats, "Let the redeemed of the Lord say so." As we unpack what God has redeemed and what He longs to redeem in your life right now, can you position and prepare yourself for this declaration today?

To the Wanderer, whether you feel lost in your calling or in your purpose, it's not a matter that will be solved with time, but rather with a decision to call on God immediately. Psalm 107:4 says, ***"Some wandered in desert wastelands, finding no way to a city where they could settle."*** Then verses 6-7 say, ***"Then they cried out to the Lord in their trouble, and He delivered them from their distress. He led them by a straight way to a city where they could settle."*** God is a God of direction, plan, and purpose, we just need to give Him our map. As you choose to follow His lead today, declare your redemption!

To the guilt-ridden: the choices that you've made in your own self-interest no longer have to define or paralyze you. Verse 10 says, **"Some sat in darkness, in utter darkness, prisoners suffering in iron chains."** But they chose not to stay there. Verse 13-14, **"Then they cried to the Lord in their trouble, and He saved them from their distress. He brought them out of the darkness, the utter darkness, and broke away their chains."** God doesn't just reach down to those on the surface, but He reaches to the furthest depths of darkness to redeem His girls who call out to Him. As your eyes adjust to the light of His love, declare your redemption!

To the hurting: it doesn't take but a moment in the presence of sickness to become infected. In our world, it doesn't take much for us to become sick and weak on its disease to please and the desire to gain more and more. Most often, we don't know that we are sick until we are battling its painful symptoms. In verse 17, **"Some became fools through their rebellious ways and suffered affliction because of their iniquities."** But our God is bigger than our sickness. Verse 19-20, **"Then they cried to the Lord in their trouble, and He saved them from their distress."** God's presence is the remedy and His love puts what's broken back together. As you come to the Healer, you get to declare yourself redeemed!

To the sea-sick: most likely you didn't ask for the storms in your life. You are tired of the crashing waves and the never-ending sway. Verse 23, **"Some went out on the sea in ships."** A reminder that we can go willingly and obediently, but there will never be a guarantee of manageable waters. Verse 26, **"They (waves) mounted up to the heavens and went down to the depths; in their peril their courage melted away."** Verse 28, **"Then they cried out to the Lord in their trouble, and He brought them out of their distress."** Calming the seas is not our job, but the Lord's. Performing a miracle is out of our wheelhouse. So we must take our eyes off of the waves and fix them on the Storm-Tamer. As we do this, we find redemption in our hardest seasons, so let's declare it!

"Let the redeemed of the Lord tell their story—those He redeemed from the hand of the foe, those He gathered from the lands, from east and west, from north and south." Psalm 107:2-3

The most important work that you may ever do is to share the story of your redemption. Because God in His mercy can redeem it, our job is to declare it. The greatest disservice that we can give is to make people believe that we've survived in our own strength. In our wandering, in our guilt, in our sickness, and in the storms of life, we are never alone. That is the story that is worth sharing. All you who have been redeemed, SAY SO!

God, we don't deserve You but Your Son makes us worthy, and in Your great love You rescue us to tell Your story. May we never take the credit for the rescue. Thank You for Psalm 107, for all of the stories of redemption behind us, and all of the stories of redemption up ahead. We trust You with today! We love You. Amen.

78

USE WEARY FOR GOOD

. . . .

"Our own personal weariness should serve
as our reminder to do good for one another."

Michelle Myers

"Let us not become weary in doing good, for at the proper time we will reap a harvest if we do not give up." Galatians 6:9

No doubt, you've probably turned to this verse dozens of times for encouragement. After all, it's hard to keep doing good when you feel unnoticed or unappreciated.

Or maybe it's just that you feel like, compared with how hard you're working, the harvest isn't big enough or it isn't coming quick enough.

Feel familiar?

Well, here's some good news. The Bible doesn't stop there. Examine the next verse:

"Therefore, as we have opportunity, let us do good to all people, especially to those who belong to the family of believers." Galatians 6:10

"Therefore" is our indicator that these two verses are connected. Whenever you come across the word "therefore" in God's Word, it should serve as your reminder to look back at what comes before. (*My pastor growing up used to always say, "Always ask, "What's 'therefore' there for?"*)

So why is therefore there? To instruct us that, because it's easy to grow weary in doing good, we should do good to everyone, especially to other believers.

Our own personal weariness should serve as our reminder to do good for one another.

So here's our question:

If you know that you grow weary in doing good, what are you actively doing to encourage others who are doing good so they won't grow weary?

Basically, what are you doing to help others live out God's calling on their lives?

It's easy to get self-absorbed…*even* in faith-based work. Selfishness isn't always intentional.

Selfishness, however, is what we default to, unless we purposefully pursue selflessness. And selflessness doesn't occur accidentally.

So the next time you find yourself growing weary in doing good, rather than considering quitting or merely wallowing in your own weariness, do good for someone else.

Serve someone.

Pray with someone.

Promote someone else.

You never know how the smallest act of encouragement could impact someone in your life.

You'll likely never be able to make living God's calling on your own life easier… but you can make the choice to lighten someone else's load.

Let's make that choice. You in?

God, thank You for Your Word. Forgive me for how many times I've made these verses about me and my own personal weariness. You've positioned me in the lives of others. I'm not here by accident. God, don't let me default to selfishness, but help me selflessly pursue a life that encourages others and eases the load for those around me. God, give me Your eyes to see the needs of those around me and Your strength to meet those needs. Help me to use my own weariness as a reminder not to quit, but to serve those around me. I love You. Amen.

79

BE STRONG AND COURAGEOUS

. . . .

"Our surrender releases the power of God to act on our behalf."

Liz Patton

After the death of Moses, I [Liz] think you would probably agree with me that Joshua had some pretty big shoes to fill in order to get the Israelites safely across the Jordan River into the Promised Land. That is why I love it so much that God reassures Joshua and gives him this little pep talk in Joshua 1:5-7:

"No one will be able to stand up against you all the days of your life. As I was with Moses, so I will be with you; I will never leave you or forsake you. Be strong and courageous, because you will lead these people to inherit the land I swore to their forefathers to give them. Be strong and very courageous."

With the ark of the covenant leading them, the Israelites all went down to the water's edge of the Jordan. Even though God had promised He would never leave them or forsake them, I can imagine the Israelites were probably still a little terrified as they looked into the deep water of the Jordan River *(which by the way was at flood stage)!*

"Yet as soon as the priests who carried the ark reached the Jordan and their feet touched the water's edge, the water from upstream stopped flowing." **Joshua 3:15**

Can you just imagine?! AS SOON AS their feet touched the water's edge, the water stopped flowing, and they crossed the Jordan on DRY ground!

I love what our pastor had to say about the Israelites' faith as they approached the water's edge: "What released God's power was their faith in His promise. What is YOUR Jordan that keeps you from plowing ahead into the life God has planned for you?"

Wow. I know, right?! I'd love for you to take a few minutes to think about that question: What is the barrier that is preventing you from stepping out in faith? What is keeping you stalled at the water's edge? What is preventing you from diving in?

Maybe it's pride, entitlement, envy, contentment, self-importance, laziness, selfishness, anger, fear, worry, doubt. Yuck. What a messy list to have to write and consider, but once we recognize what is holding us back, we can surrender it! Amen? Then our surrender releases the power of God to act on our behalf!

The other part of this story that I love and want to point out is that the priests who were carrying the ark of the covenant of the Lord *"stood firm on dry ground in the middle of the Jordan, while all Israel passed by until the whole nation had completed the crossing on dry ground."* This demonstrates that God Himself was with them in the place of danger until every single person was safely across. He never leaves us or forsakes us!

My sweet sister, you might go down to the water's edge with your knees knocking, but your good, good Father is whispering in your ear, "Be strong and courageous." He will go before you, standing in your place of danger until you're safely across whatever your Jordan might be today. All He requires of you is your step of faith. Will you jump in with Him?

Dear God, we are so thankful that You promise us that You will never leave us or forsake us. Thank You for Your protection and for acting on our behalf when we step out in faith. You are so, so good to us. We are tired of standing back, and so today with surrendered hearts, we come to the water's edge, and we dive in with You. We are so in love with You. Amen.

80

HIS WAY

· ·

"Practice + Evaluation makes perfect."

Somer Phoebus

Practice makes perfect.

Not exactly...

Practice with evaluation makes perfect.

Self-evaluation isn't easy, but every time we open God's Word we're saying "yes" to a very real and sometimes very unattractive look at ourselves. His Word is a mirror into our heart. When we read it, we see our faults and our shortcomings but we also see His promises! We see what He wants from us and we see that He doesn't expect us to do it alone.

The only way we can expect our journey with God to bring us to a place of intimacy with him is to practice doing life His way AND be open to evaluation often.

The scariest thing about modern Christianity is that people are doing a lot of practicing, but they're practicing what they believe to be the right thing. They actually believe that God can be whomever they want Him to be, that the gospel is based on opinion and the belief that what it takes to call yourself a follower of Christ is up for negotiation. So they end up practicing a "good" life, but not a "His way" life, and never recognize it – all because they never evaluate their heart based on His truth...on His Word!

Jesus said to him, "I am the way, and the truth, and the life. No one comes to the Father except through me." John 14:6

We can make good choices but miss the point. We can miss the WAY! If we're not living for Jesus, nothing we do matters! Because if it's earthly, it's fleeting. But if it's Spirit-led, it's forever! Are you practicing for the right now life or are you practicing for the eternal? How do you know? Ask the Holy Spirit! *(I know, yikes!)*

You see...
We practice
The Holy Spirit evaluates

When a Christian life is open to what the Holy Spirit reveals, adjustments happen, sin is recognized, and intimacy grows. And where there's intimacy, there will never be casual Christianity. Where there's intimacy, there's clear direction and total access to the narrow way.

"Enter by the narrow gate. For the gate is wide and the way is easy that leads to destruction, and those who enter by it are many. For the gate is narrow and the way is hard that leads to life, and those who find it are few."
Matthew 7:13-14

Don't just practice being a good Christian. Evaluate your life based on His Word! We've got to hold ourselves accountable to live out the REAL gospel, even if it's less comfortable.

Jesus, thank You for Your Holy Spirit that lives in me. Help me to recognize Your voice and to obey what You ask. God, I don't want to practice being good – I want to practice being holy. Forgive me when I fall short! I love You. Amen.

81

AS HE IS, SO ARE WE

. . . .

"Our Focus: What will the end result give me?
God's Focus: Faithfulness throughout the entire
process is the priority."

Jessica Hottle

I [Jessica] believe we have spent so much time on a business strategy to be more liked than a business strategy that shows more of His love, with the truth and the whole truth.

How can I share the gospel but also not offend anyone?
How can I share the gospel but also get more followers?
How can I share the gospel but also be liked by others?

As Michelle Myers says here in the *she works His way* community, "We should be leading with a gospel that saves not a gospel that sells."

I'm not writing to you today from a place that says I have nailed it. I'm writing to you today to say, "I get you. I've been there." But, also to tell you that there's more for you than to be liked by someone you may never ever meet in your entire life.

Social media makes it easier and easier for us to be someone we are not because we want to be like someone else. We follow them and begin to think (although maybe not consciously) that if we could do what she does, we could have what she has.

Let's see what 1 John 4:17 says: ***"This is how love is made complete among us so that we will have confidence on the day of judgment: In this world, we are like Jesus."***

As He is in this world, so are we.

As women who have hearts working His way, this should be our anthem song, our starting point.

Am I leading, loving, and living like Jesus did when He walked this earth?

He's not looking for you to be perfect or to get it right. He's looking for those who will be faithful with what they have been given today.

He's looking for women who say, "Yes, Jesus, send me. I don't know what I am doing tomorrow, but I will choose today to steward what You have blessed me with well."

"Very truly I tell you, whoever believes in me will do the works I have been doing, and they will do even greater things than these, because I am going to the Father." John 4:12

Jesus cast out demons, healed the sick, and did miracles, signs, and wonders. (All that spiritual power has also been transferred to us by the cross.) Scripture tells us we will do even greater things than that.

But, we can't do greater things than He did if we aren't willing to lead well, love well, and live well with 50 followers, or a small Bible study group that may have just started, or a new ministry you may have just launched.

We look to the end result. God is looking for our faithfulness. Let this be an encouragement to your heart, not a discouragement:

You will offend people with the whole truth and that's good news.

You may not have thousands of followers on social media like other people and that's good news.

You will not be liked by everyone and that's good news.

As He is, so are we and that's good news.

Father, we are so grateful that You search our hearts and know that we won't get it right or perfect every time. We are thankful for the cross for redemption and repentance. Help us keep our hearts open and ready to receive all of who You are with every passing day as we continue to renew our minds to lead, live, and love like You! We love You. Amen!

SHE WORKS HIS WAY

82

NOT UP FOR DEBATE

. . . .

"Your past does not get to determine your future with Jesus."

Emily Copeland

There is no doubt that when I [Emily] talk with friends who are pursuing God, one of their greatest fears is dealing with a haunting past of mistakes. They feel as though they can hear the whispers of people who knew them saying, "Isn't that her?", "Didn't she...?".

If you immediately recognize this as a tender spot in your life today, will you read the story of Mark 6:1-5 with me?

Jesus left there and went to his hometown, accompanied by his disciples. When the Sabbath came, he began to teach in the synagogue, and many who heard him were amazed. "Where did this man get these things?" they asked. "What's this wisdom that has been given him? What are these remarkable miracles he is performing? Isn't this the carpenter? Isn't this Mary's son and the brother of James, Joseph, Judas and Simon? Aren't his sisters here with us?" And they took offense at him. Jesus said to them, "A prophet is not without honor except in his own town, among his relatives and in his own home." He could not do any miracles there, except lay his hands on a few sick people and heal them.

In my Bible, this portion of Scripture is titled, "A Prophet without Honor." The disbelief of the people in Jesus' hometown came from a place of familiarity. They felt like they knew Him too well, so there was just no way that He could be the Messiah that He claimed to be. Familiarity can cloud our judgement at times, causing us to question what we know even when we've been given a new assignment that has been delivered with grace and forgiveness.

Can we say that Jesus' neighbors were way out of line? Maybe, but consider how this would look in your life if a neighbor in your community were to proclaim something so bold? In our human hearts and minds, our rationale would kick in and tell us that something isn't right. But Jesus' goal was never to win every heart with rationality, but with love and truth. Many of these neighbors accepted Christ before the end of their lives, understanding that Jesus' life was unconventional from the very start. And, I can imagine that you may say the same about your own life.

Your faith, regardless of your past, is not designed for everyone to understand. But, your job is to live it out regardless of who is watching so that Jesus can work in every moment that you're here.

Any lack of faith on their part in what God may be doing in your life has zero bearing on your God-given calling. If you hesitate because of what those people from your past may think, then you are entering the dangerous waters of disobedience.

"Anyone, then, who know the good that he ought to do and doesn't do it, sins." James 4:17

People cannot disqualify you. Your history cannot disqualify you. Your past does not get to determine your future with Jesus.

Jesus has determined us worthy of the work because of His own sacrifice.

"I have been crucified with Christ and I no longer live, but Christ lives in me. The life I now live in the body, I live by faith in the Son of God, who loved me and gave himself for me." Galatians 2:20.

So when people say, "didn't she...?" you can confidently say, "Yes, then Jesus..."

God, in our moments of fear and hesitation to continue moving forward in the call that You've given only to us, remind us that, all throughout history, You've been changing our past and equipping us for the future. Help us not to worry about what people may say or think. But instead, fill us up with Your strength so that we can effectively point all eyes to Your glory. We love You. Amen.

83

WELCOME INTERRUPTION

. . . .

"If we are more committed to our systems and automation
than we are to people, we cannot claim to be
ministry-minded. People are the point of ministry."

Michelle Myers

I [Michelle] despise multi-tasking. Maybe it's because, for so many years, I wore it like a badge of honor. Over time, I've learned that multi-tasking is fine for menial tasks, but important things require focus.

But people always trump tasks...even if those tasks are important. Even missional tasks.

Jesus gives us a beautiful example of this in Mark 5. *(I'd love for you to read Mark 5:21-43 on your own!)*

Jairus, a synagogue official, came to Jesus in desperation when his 12-year-old daughter was sick and about to die. He begged Jesus to come heal her.

As they walked together to Jairus' house with a huge crowd following them, a woman who had been bleeding for 12 years knew that if she were able to touch Jesus, she could be healed. So when He walked by her, she touched His cloak, and she was healed immediately.

This woman was constantly overlooked; she was an outcast of society for being ceremonially unclean because of her condition. Given who she was and that the text tells us that the crowds were pressing in on Him (Mark 5:24), she probably wouldn't have even been offended if Jesus hadn't noticed or stopped.

But He did.

"Who touched my garments?" Jesus asked (Mark 5:31).

Fearful, she came before Jesus and told Him the whole story. As He responded to her that her faith had made her well and to go in peace and be healed, someone from Jairus' house came to let them know his daughter had died (Mark 5:34-35).

Then, an already good story, turns into an amazing story, as Jesus continues to Jairus' house and brings the little girl back to life (Mark 5:42).

Honestly, it seems kind of random to interrupt the flow of Jesus' miracle of healing this little girl...unless we're supposed to learn something from Jesus' example.

We're *she works His way* women. We're focused. We're on a mission. We have a job to do, and because of our commitment to living a priority-based life, we don't have a ton of time to do it.

But are we ever so focused that we don't notice the "unrelated" needs around us?
- The children's class at church that needs a teacher once a month?

- The school administrative assistant you always rush past as you're heading back to your car who always looks like she's about to cry?

- Your kid's friend who doesn't have a good home life?

Needs are all around us. This is a hurting world. A world that is desperately trying all sorts of solutions that will never satisfy...and we have the only Answer that ever will.

We talk about this all the time here, but it's worth saying again: **People cannot be automated or systematized, and people are the point of ministry.** If we are more committed to our systems and automation than people, we cannot claim to be ministry-minded.

Dave Earley defines ministry as "getting dirty to make others clean." And getting dirty implies we will have to welcome an interruption or two into our lives.

But here's the beautiful part: Whenever I allow God to interrupt my day, I typically end up being the one who is radically blessed because I get to witness Him at work. If I live and die by my schedule alone, I may miss the best thing He had planned for my day.

There's nothing wrong with focus, and there's still plenty of time for that. But as we go about our callings and responsibilities, let's make sure we have a pliable posture where God knows He can interrupt us to do His work.

Because can't we trust that we can do more with Him than we could ever do on our most productive day without Him?

Let's prove it.

God, forgive me when I act in such a way that values tasks over people. God, I know that You have a deep love for all of Your children. Help me to see others as You do. Give me Your heart for them. Burden me to see the needs of others and to be Your hands and feet whenever I can. Help me to act more as a doer for Your Kingdom, not merely to function in an earthly position this world can identify. I love you! Amen.

84

IMMEDIATE CHANGE

. . . .

*"The very act of salvation requires complete surrender,
so it's absolutely ridiculous that we would give God part of us
and expect Him to fill us with ALL of Himself in return."*

Somer Phoebus

We often refer to our walk with Christ as a journey. Nothing could be more true! The more I [Somer] experience my Savior, the more I love Him, need Him, and want to serve Him. That's the journey of many relationships, but especially of the one between a human and her Heavenly Father.

But there are parts about our walks with Christ that are also instant, and it's important that we realize what those are. We can't "bank" on these things being a process or a progression. We can't use the explanation of our "journey" with Christ as an out for our sin. e.g. "I'm just doing my best to get better day by day - eventually I'll live the life of a holy woman."

I love this quote by Oswald Chambers:

"We do not grow into a spiritual relationship step by step, we either have a relationship or we do not."

And to have a relationship means that there has been instant transformation. We have met with God, and we have handed our lives over to Him. In that moment these two things should be instant...

Surrender
The very act of salvation requires complete surrender. It is absolutely ridiculous that we would give God part of us and expect Him to fill us with ALL of Himself in return. But I see it all the time. We do it with our time, we do it with our money, and we do it with our gifts: "God, this is what I can give you now but I'm working on more!" That doesn't fly. Jesus laid down His WHOLE life for us. The least we can do is lay down our EVERYTHING for Him. **Romans 12:1**

When Jesus met Paul on the Road to Damascus, He sent Ananias to Paul and Ananias was not about to let Paul tiptoe into surrender!

And he said, 'The God of our fathers appointed you to know his will, to see the Righteous One and to hear a voice from his mouth; for you will be a witness for him to everyone of what you have seen and heard. And now why do you wait? Rise and be baptized and wash away your sins, calling on his name.' Acts 22:14-16

Obedience
We should desire to obey Him in every way and immediately. We don't get to slow roll into it. There's no practicing obedience. Also, we need to understand that nowhere in Scripture does it tell us God's voice is quieter or harder to make out in the beginning of our walk with Him. Once we give Him our hearts, He takes residence there and the Holy Spirit will speak loud and clear…if we listen. Paul had an INSTANT transformation that resulted in an INSTANT desire to be obedient. He went from murdering Christians one day to proclaiming God the next, all because he obeyed IMMEDIATELY.

And immediately he proclaimed Jesus in the synagogues, saying, "He is the Son of God." Acts 9:20

So yes, there is a journey. Our journey with God is one that will be equally challenging and rewarding. However, in order for our journey to move forward, we must immediately, and with all that we are, surrender our WHOLE lives and walk in obedience! The salvation experience is an instant transformation and we must never forget that! We must never forget the power in that moment we first believed. Our transformation to being made a new creation will produce a desire to instantly surrender and obey!

"Therefore, if anyone is in Christ, he is a new creation. The old has passed away; behold, the new has come." 2 Corinthians 5:17

God, I surrender everything I am. I want to be obedient to what You ask of me. Thank You for the gift of salvation! Thank You for the transformation You bring to my life when You place Your Holy Spirit in me. Lord, I don't want to be a casual follower of You, but instead let me live like the NEW CREATURE You made me to be the moment I first believed! I love You. Amen.

85

WE WIN!

. . . .

"We need to remember that people are not our problem. Satan is."

Liz Patton

Recently, I [Liz] was taking a cycle class and the instructor said, "Because we know what's coming next, we can sit in our confidence." What she meant was that, because we had already done that particular drill, we could be confident on our bikes the next time we did it, since we knew what to expect. We knew we would succeed.

As I drove home from the gym, I kept replaying that quote in my mind and realized the same is true in our lives too. Because we know what's coming next (and even more importantly, because we know Who wins in the end) as followers of Jesus, we can sit in our confidence! And that, my sweet friends, is some Good News to get pumped up about today; am I right?!

"Then war broke out in heaven. Michael and his angels fought against the dragon, and the dragon and his angels fought back. But he was not strong enough, and they lost their place in heaven. The great dragon was hurled down—that ancient serpent called the devil, or Satan, who leads the whole world astray. He was hurled to the earth, and his angels with him." Revelation 12:7-9

I'm no theologian, and I wouldn't even begin to try and explain the book of Revelation. But I know who wins in the end, and that allows me to sit in my confidence!

I think where this gets tricky for us is that we get bogged down by things in our physical world without realizing that everything physical is influenced by something spiritual. We need to remember that people are not our problem. Satan is.

Your problem is not with your spouse who misunderstands you.
Your problem is not with your belligerent child.

187

SHE WORKS HIS WAY

Your problem is not with your grumpy co-worker.
Your problem is not with the driver who cuts in front of you in traffic.
Your problem is not with your selfish neighbor.
Your problem is not with an overbearing, critical, or absent parent.
Your problem is not with your friend who gossips.

Because people are not the problem, we need to stop fighting them as if they are the problem! When we do that, the enemy wins. Let's face it – it's harder to defeat something that we cannot see, but that's exactly why we need to let God fight for us! How do we do that? By putting on the full armor of God:

"Finally, be strong in the Lord and in his mighty power. Put on the full armor of God, so that you can take your stand against the devil's schemes. For our struggle is not against flesh and blood, but against the rulers, against the authorities, against the powers of this dark world and against the spiritual forces of evil in the heavenly realms. Therefore put on the full armor of God, so that when the day of evil comes, you may be able to stand your ground, and after you have done everything, to stand." **Ephesians 6:10-13**

Sister, today let's sit in confidence, letting our God fight for us, because we know that in the end, He wins.

Dear God, we are so grateful that we're on Your team. Your Word reminds us that we have conquered the enemy by the blood of the Lamb and by the word of our testimony (Rev. 12:10-11). Thank You for Your sacrifice on the cross that has saved us from our sins. Please give us a boldness to share our testimony with others so that they can be drawn to You. We are putting on our armor today as we find our strength in You. Thank You for fighting for us. We love You. Amen.

188

86

GOD'S JOB

. . . .

"God's job through us, not our job through God."

Emily Copeland

As I'm [Emily] typing, I'm looking out through my bedroom window towards the back of the house which sits in front of a field. I can see the perfect amount of snow falling from the sky, and the entire area is just lightly covered in snow. It looks like a painting. But as I look out at this landscape, you would rightfully call me insane for claiming that the snow-covered field was my creation. Of course, I didn't create the snow or the field, but in what other areas of my life am I trying to take credit for a product or result only God could create?

One of my all-time favorite stories in the Bible can be found at the end of Genesis. In Chapter 40, you'll find a cupbearer and a baker asking Joseph to interpret their dreams. God had given Joseph the ability to interpret dreams, and these men were looking for help. Like so many of us, Joseph could have easily said, "Oh, I can do that!", but instead, his response was, "Do not interpretations belong to God?" (v. 8)

In other words, Joseph knew his job was to deliver. He was the message bearer, not the hero of the story. He was given the ability to interpret dreams as a gift and could only be of service when God gave him the information.

Joseph knew the equation well: God's job through him, not his job through God.

Here is where I'm afraid we get it wrong (and I know this first-hand). We are given an opportunity to step in and help, and so we recruit God into the mix when we need Him. We ask Him to bless our efforts and to make them fruitful, but we assume too much of the role for ourselves. We end up settling for our own ideas instead of inviting God to just do His work through us. Ultimately, we make a statement with our life that our work is more important than His work through us.

How do we know if God is working through us, or if we are working through God? Let's start with some simple questions:

Have you prayed more than you've planned?
For God to do a job through us, we have to position ourselves before Him. Yes, planning takes a lot of time and effort, but prayer clarifies your direction and confirms the work at hand.

Have your ideas come from time spent with God or apart from God?
I'm not saying that every idea or assignment comes from time spent in prayer, but I will say that moments in prayer will confirm them. If all of your ideas have come from your own reflections and not from a collaboration of prayer, God's Word, and time around hurting people, then it may just be a "you" idea and not a "God" assignment.

Do you find yourself asking God to bless your efforts, or bless your obedience?
Many times, we make a decision and start working on it and then invite God in to make it grow or succeed. But if we are asking God to bless our obedience, then it means that our starting place is rooted in faith and we have chosen to follow God's lead, not our own.

So let's examine our starting point. Is it a dream that we've had on our hearts and hope that God will bring it to life? Or, is our dream that God would work through us in any capacity?

Even from being wrongfully thrown in prison for years, God worked through Joseph. I can imagine that he wouldn't have chosen prison for himself, but I'm sure he quickly realized that there was no better place to be as God worked through him to change the course of history.

It is never too late to surrender your life, your plans, and your dreams to God. He knows what's on your heart, and many times God does use our dreams to get His job done. But, we have to be fully flexible to be a vessel for His work at any given time. Just think of what it's like to be used by God, and to be so intimately involved with Kingdom work! Friends, no earthly dream compares.

God, we are so grateful to be used by You. The word "privilege" just feels too small. It is the blessing of our lives to be involved in Your work. Help us not to miss this today. Help us to be willing to lay it all aside and to begin aching to be used by You in any capacity. We are ready to be used by You today! We love You. Amen.

87

HE IS ENOUGH

. . . .

"He must be enough before we ever try to make enough."

Jessica Hottle

Exodus 14:14 says, **"The Lord will fight for you; you need only to be still."** At the time Moses said this, the Israelites were about to cross the Red Sea, from slavery into freedom as they watched God part the sea and kill the very men that kept them captive.

Fast forward to Numbers 12:7-9 which says, **"[My servant Moses] is faithful in all my house. I speak with him face to face, even plainly, and not in dark sayings; and he sees the form of the Lord. Why then were you not afraid to speak against my servant Moses? So, the anger of the Lord was aroused against them."** At this time, Aaron and Miriam were gossiping about Moses and the wife he married and questioning if Moses is the only one that the Lord has spoken through.

The point of these two Scriptures is simple: He does what He says He will do. Period.

The Lord fought for His servant Moses. The Lord was angry that they were speaking against him. The Lord came to Moses' defense.

And guess what? He's doing the same for you.

In business, motherhood, relationships…in every part of your life He's saying, "I will fight for you on your behalf. You are my daughter with whom I am well pleased."

As I [Jessica] read through the journey of the Israelites passing through the wilderness one thing stands true: He must always be enough.

Countless times when the Lord didn't act quickly enough in their eyes, they acted themselves, creating idols, going into battle without the Lord, or trying to get other leaders to step up. The Lord was never enough for them. His promises weren't enough and the countless times He carried them through or heard their cries or how He brought them out of slavery all wasn't enough.

191

Regardless of God and His past history of faithfulness, the Israelites always wanted more proof. Then, when the Lord moved, they repented every time.

Let's take this and apply it to our business: He must be enough before we make enough.

God has a great resume, past history report, and perfect credit score in your life when you take a moment to see how He's bringing it full circle for His glory and His timing.

Take heart, my dear, sweet friend, He's fighting for you. He's standing up to the enemy on your behalf. Stand still, stand firm, and let Him do what He says He will do.

Father, I'm offering up all that I have to You today. My feelings, my emotions, and the very things or people that try to (or I let) derail me from Your purpose. Today, I am stepping aside, giving You back the reins, and letting You do what only You can do.

88

BROKEN SPIRIT

. . . .

"The sacrifices of God are a broken spirit;
a broken and contrite heart, O God, you will not despise."
Psalm 51:17

Liz Patton

Recently one of our boys had a little "mishap," and the wall in our upstairs hallway ended up with a rather large hole in it. He immediately came to us and offered to take money out of his bank account to cover the expenses to have it fixed. He even offered to do extra chores to make up for it.

As disappointed as we were about his carelessness, I [Liz] have to say that what touched my heart the most was not his offer to pay to have it fixed, but rather his broken spirit and humility in asking for our forgiveness.

And then, the very next day I was reading in Psalms and found this little gem:

"For you will not delight in sacrifice, or I would give it;
    you will not be pleased with a burnt offering.
The sacrifices of God are a broken spirit;
    a broken and contrite heart, O God, you will not despise."
Psalm 51:16-17

What a good, good Father to use His Word in such a timely way!

Now if you're thinking to yourself that you've never done anything as big or bad as putting a hole in your Father's house...well, here's the thing, my sweet friend... as daughters of the King, it's not IF we sin, but rather WHEN we sin:

"as it is written:
'None is righteous, no, not one;
    no one understands;
    no one seeks for God.

All have turned aside; together they have become worthless;
  no one does good,
  not even one.'"
Romans 3:10-12

But we don't have to allow this to dishearten us because God has given us instructions for when we sin. He just wants our "broken and contrite hearts."

After reading that piece of Scripture, I looked up the words "broken" and "contrite" to get a clearer meaning.

Broken: changing direction abruptly

Contrite: caused by or showing sincere remorse

So when we sin, we need to change directions immediately. That means we can't stay in our sin! When we feel that conviction of the Holy Spirit, we can't ignore it or justify it. We need to go the other way right now.

Once we have changed direction, we then need to show genuine remorse. There is nothing we can give God that can make it right – except for our humble hearts.

And I love the reassurance He gives us as our Father in **Psalm 103:10-13:**

"He does not deal with us according to our sins,
  nor repay us according to our iniquities.
For as high as the heavens are above the earth,
  so great is his steadfast love toward those who fear him;
as far as the east is from the west,
  so far does he remove our transgressions from us.
As a father shows compassion to his children,
  so the Lord shows compassion to those who fear him."

Dear God, please forgive us when we don't seek You, when we turn aside, and when we mess up. We know that nothing we can give You can make it right except for our broken and contrite hearts. We offer our hearts to You today as we turn from our sin. Thank You for the gift of Your Son, Jesus, who takes away our sins and washes us whiter than snow. We love You. Amen.

89

JOY VS. HAPPINESS

. . . .

"Your earthly life does not have to be miserable,
but it should not satisfy you."

Michelle Myers

Happiness. We don't usually think of happiness as an enemy. And it's not bad to be happy. But sometimes, happiness can be dangerous because it can appear similar to joy...but happiness and joy are drastically different.

For example, I [Michelle] can be happy about the win at work, when my kids are perfectly behaved, when the date night with my husband goes exactly as planned, or when the perfect stranger extends the kindest compliment.

But what happens when the deal falls through?

When my kids disappoint me?

When my spouse and I get into an argument?

When my friend uses her words for her gain and my loss?

Those things can *(and should – we are human, after all!)*, at least momentarily, steal my happiness. But they can't take my joy.

That's because joy has nothing to do with my earthly situation and has everything to do with my eternal security, which *cannot* change once Christ has captured my life.

Happiness results merely from what happens to us. JOY results from the pursuit of what happens *FOR* us.

And did you catch that subtle other difference? Happiness is cause and effect. Joy is a pursuit.

Read these words from the apostle Paul:

**"For to me, to live is Christ and to die is gain. If I am to go on living in the body, this will mean fruitful labor for me. Yet what shall I choose? I do not know! I am torn between the two: I desire to depart and be with Christ, which is better by far; but it is more necessary for you that I remain in the body. Convinced of this, I know that I will remain, and I will continue with all of you for your progress and joy in the faith, so that through my being with you again your boasting in Christ Jesus will abound on account of me."
Philippians 1:21-26**

Oh, these words have challenged me since the first time I read them. For years, I just thought, *"Okay, I'm not there yet. I have a lot to live for! I have a lot left to do!"*

But in the last year, I remember reading these words and writing a note in my Bible margins that simply said: "If you're not anxious to meet Christ, you're probably not really living for Him."

Let that sink in: If you're not longing for heaven, you're not *really* living. Because life *IS* Christ!

Now, I don't know where you are. But what I do know is this – whether you are happy or unhappy – Heaven is better!

And happiness in the absence of joy is *empty*, and joy in the absence of happiness is *everything*.

Now let me be clear: I think this idea is often misunderstood that somehow the Christian life is supposed to be miserable.

But hear me: **Your earthly life does not have to be miserable, but it should not satisfy you.**

I'm reading a book right now called *Letters to the Church* by Francis Chan, and I cannot recommend it enough. I've got a quote from it displayed in my office right now that I'm in the process of making permanent. It says this:

"I will be facing Him soon, so I have to stay focused on His desires." Francis Chan

The clock is ticking. This life isn't everything. Not even close. And God is real. SO very real. And on a day that we can't predict, we *will* face Him. And we must pursue Him *now*.

Let's refuse to settle for fleeting happiness when full joy is offered.

God, thank You for making our joy complete. Not because of our lives, God, but because of the life Jesus lived as our example and the death He died in our place. Please give me the discernment to know the difference between joy and happiness. I know You give us good gifts to enjoy in this life, but I don't want to live merely for the gifts. I want to live for the Giver, which is You. Use me while I'm here on earth, but help me live each day in anticipation of seeing You face-to-face. I love You. Amen.

90

TRUTH CLARIFIED

"Culture is the opposite of the gospel and will never be able to determine the validity of it."

Somer Phoebus

Have you ever gotten something in your eye that caused you to be unable to see or even open your eye for an extended time? Is there anything more annoying than not being able to see clearly? It happened to me [Somer] once, and of course I was driving. I guess the wise choice would have been to pull over, but I decided to forge on with my one eye. I found myself constantly trying to reopen my eye in hopes that whatever it was would be gone, but no luck. Thirty minutes of this passed and I grew SO irritated!

"Truth must be defined and safeguarded otherwise people will walk off into error. So, if we object to doctrine, it is not surprising if we do not see things clearly, it is not surprising if we are unhappy and miserable." **D. Martyn Lloyd-Jones**

We live in a pretty miserable world and there are a lot of reasons for that. But I think the overarching reason is our inability to see and submit to truth – and nothing is more frustrating than not being able to see truth clearly. It's like living in this long term state of confusion. We bring it on ourselves though. Constantly reexamining over and over again what we know to be of God because we want to be sure that it is, or because we want to prove that it isn't. That right there is a symptom of poor "sight."

Maybe we should stop examining God, and spend a little more time examining our own hearts.

Our desire for truth is something we were born with, which is why we're pretty uncomfortable when we don't recognize it. But that desire is also met with a fleshly desire to live comfortably and blaze our own trail. So we begin to pick and choose the parts we want to believe as they relate to our own plans and needs. We justify this by telling ourselves God loves us so much He wants us to be happy.

But you've heard it before and I'm going to tell you again: God's desire is not for us to be happy, but for us to be holy. And that requires living a life that believes and submits to His truth.

In my experience, the more I try to convince myself of something, the less true it probably is. Do you find yourself constantly wanting to debunk some portion of Scripture because, if you acknowledged it as true, you would have to change something in your life? That's a red flag!

We're so good at justifying ourselves when we put our "truth" above the truth in Scripture! We argue so well!

"Did God really mean that literally or can I leave it up to my own interpretation?"

"Oh, this command was obviously meant for people who lived in Bible times."

"This part can't be right because if I live this way or do this thing, I will offend people and God wouldn't want that."

Guys, do you understand that there are actually people *(false teachers)* who are teaching that we need to examine Scripture through the eyes of today's culture before we define it? That's like sending a dentist to examine someone's eyes. Culture is the opposite of the gospel and will never determine the validity of it – and I don't know a better way to put this so I'm just going to say it: Culture is dumb. Culture is determined by humans and humans are LOST without Jesus.

Here at *she works His way*, we believe in the Bible totally and completely. We believe the feel-good stories, but we also recognize the parts that call us out, step on our toes, and remind us of a God who loves us more than anything and who should also be feared. We believe it is 100% TRUE!

As you go to Bible studies and listen to podcast sermons, or go to conferences and sit under the teaching of others, will you make sure that what they are teaching aligns with truth? And if you find yourself confused about what truth is, will you take it to Scripture? It's so incredibly important.

We must define and safeguard the truth. Otherwise WE will be the people who walk off into error, and I don't want to be the generation that allows that to happen anymore than it already has.

Jesus, show us the way! Show us the truth by giving us a deep craving to know it. Give us wisdom to discern what is of You and what is not. Forgive us for being worried about offending someone or causing controversy. God, help us to see what is at stake if we don't stand for Your truth. We love You so much! Amen.

91

CHOSEN

. . . .

"When we proclaim God's Word and speak His truth, we can be
assured that it will do its work. The Word is what does the work."

Jessica Hottle

*"Praise be to the God and Father of our Lord Jesus Christ, who has blessed
us in the heavenly realms with every spiritual blessing in Christ. For He chose
us in Him before the creation of the world to be holy and blameless in His
sight. In love He predestined us for adoption to sonship through Jesus Christ,
in accordance with His pleasure and will—to the praise of His glorious grace,
which He has freely given us in the One he loves. In Him we have redemption
through His blood, the forgiveness of sins, in accordance with the riches of
God's grace that He lavished on us. With all wisdom and understanding, He
made known to us the mystery of His will according to His good pleasure,
which He purposed in Christ, to be put into effect when the times reach their
fulfillment—to bring unity to all things in Heaven and on earth under Christ.*

*In Him we were also chosen, having been predestined according to the plan
of Him who works out everything in conformity with the purpose of His
will, in order that we, who were the first to put our hope in Christ, might be
for the praise of His glory. And you also were included in Christ when you
heard the message of truth, the gospel of your salvation. When you believed,
you were marked in Him with a seal, the promised Holy Spirit, who is a
deposit guaranteeing our inheritance until the redemption of those who are
God's possession—to the praise of his glory." Ephesians 1:3-14*

Paul tells us that we are:
- In Christ
- Holy and blameless
- Chosen
- Adopted as sons and daughters of God
- Forgiven

Paul also tells us that we have been given:
- Knowledge of the mysteries of God
- A purpose to live for God's praise
- The Holy Spirit

I [Jessica] believe we get so focused on begging God to move on our behalf that we forget what He has already given to us.

Our focus becomes on what we need to do instead of what God has already done for us in Christ, especially His death on the cross.

It's easier to rely on our senses (what we can touch, see, smell, hear, and feel) more than to rely on God's Word. We begin to believe that if we haven't seen it happen yet then it must not exist. But God's Word doesn't work like that. And, if we are being honest, neither does our faith.

Just because you don't see it in your experience doesn't mean it doesn't spiritually exist.

What God has said about you and the promises He has for you are real even if you can't "see" them yet. It's knowing that His Word never returns void. When we proclaim God's Word and speak His truth, we can be assured that it will do its work.

The Word is what does the work.

Once we understand what we have been given, our prayer life begins to change. What we once begged God for, we can now release in prayer.

When you are working God's way, His Word should trump any business training, launch that didn't go as planned, discouragement from people on social media, or people who try to convince you that you are crazy to run your business that way.

The words spoken about you and to you and the business adventures that didn't go as planned may be real, but they are not the truth about who you are (unless, of course, they align with God's Word).

It's normal for us not to get it right all the time. We have an enemy who is seeking to devour us, destroy us, and steal from us, and he will do anything to keep us from spreading the gospel, especially through our businesses/ministries.

Before believing anything anyone says to you or anything that happens to you, ask yourself, "Does this align with God's Word and His truth for my life?" Also ask yourself, "Is this God's nature and heart?"

Much of what we believe about ourselves and our business is based on other opinions versus the truth.

Can we be women who have hearts that go to the Word first instead of the world?

I believe it's time to ask yourself (take inventory on) what you have been believing, and then get rid of everything that isn't His truth.

Father, I know that I lack nothing with You. I have been given every spiritual blessing. Help me to discern the truth when others speak into me. Show me the areas in my life where I need to renew my mind in Your truth. Let me focus on what You have done more than on what I need. I love You. Amen!

92

WHEN GOD CALLS

. . . .

"It matters most Who calls you, not who approves of your calling."

Emily Copeland

Regardless of whether or not you have taken the enneagram test, I [Emily] feel like it's important for me to confess that I'm a nine which is known as the "Peacemaker." Ultimately, this test would describe me in my healthiest moments as an encourager, supporter, sympathizer, and a helper when it comes to easing tension-filled situations. In my unhealthiest moments, I get insecure, needy, overwhelmed, and withdrawn (Do you want to be my friend?)

When a new decision or opportunity arises in my life, I have a very deep-seated instinct to share it with everyone that I know and then try to somehow take everyone's advice so that they are happy with my decision. What's worse, I allow the words of people to either validate my decision or to make me feel like I've totally blown it.

This can get really, REALLY tricky when God is clearly calling me to something. I find boosts of energy to obey, but can quickly feel deflated under the opinions of others or the calling that God has given someone else. The biggest problem, however, is not my confusion, but in whom I am trusting: either myself or God. In my searching and wandering, I am desperate to represent myself in the best light with the best plan that everyone will approve of. God does not get the glory because, at times, I don't bring Him into it.

It didn't take but a moment in Galatians chapter one for me to feel the weight of Paul's choices to follow God versus my choices to allow confusion in.

Here are the facts:

1. Paul was sent by God, not by man. ***"Paul, an apostle-sent not from men nor by a man, but by Jesus Christ and God the Father, who raised him from the dead." Galatians 1:1***

It matters most Who calls you, not who approves of your calling.

The job that we've been given has ultimately not been given by man, but from God. Did a man or woman hire you? Great! They are part of God's plan. Did God give you an entrepreneurial spirit? Good! The vision came from Him. Are you at home raising children? Incredible. God has graced you with this role (you cannot blame it on your husband!). Paul knew WHO sent Him. We must listen for His voice and follow, then we must remember that God orchestrated it and He is trustworthy.

2. Paul consulted God first, not man. *"I did not go up to Jerusalem to see those who were apostles before I was, but I went into Arabia. Later returned to Damascus." Galatians 1:17*

In this time right after his life-changing encounter with God, Paul spent time isolated, allowing God to shape his mission. How often do we isolate ourselves from others in the moment in order to hear what God wants out of the mission? When we are in the decision-making process, we tend to be more vulnerable to being swayed side to side. Remember, the advice of our friends and family may be helpful, but when God speaks, it's purpose-filled.

3. The Result: Man could see God's hand in Paul's life. *"They only heard the report: 'The man who formerly persecuted us is now preaching the faith he once tried to destroy.' And they praised God because of me." Galatians 1:23-24.*

Because Paul knew that God sent him and then chose to allow God to influence and mold the mission, man could see God in and through Paul. Imagine if Paul had been on the road to Damascus, met God, then went straight to his buddies and asked them what they thought that he should do? How often do we do this?

Friend, if God has called you, get in His presence and beg Him to lead the way and protect your heart against the voices that will speak up at some point in the journey.

How can we see God's hand moving in us if we only consult our friends? How can our friends see God move in us if we don't consult with Him? Our life's purpose is ABOUT people, but it's not given to us by people or confirmed by people. Remember WHO has called you and lean into His voice with every step. Allow friends to encourage and support you – that is their role and that is a GIFT. But, leave your life's plan up to God.

God, forgive me for the moments that I've leaned into the thoughts and opinions of people rather than You, the One Who holds the entire plan. Help me to fix my eyes on You today and to remember that Paul's faithfulness to trust his Source led to a life of eternal rewards with You and Kingdom impact for others. Thank You for being our Guide, Provider, Sustainer, and Deliverer. We love You. Amen.

93

OBEDIENCE = BLESSING

. . . .

*"So often we turn to a self-help book or call a friend when
what we really need to do is just cry out to Jesus."*

Liz Patton

In this crazy, competitive world that we live in, it's easy to think that if we want more success, we just need to put forth more effort and more striving, write more to-do lists, or create a more detailed business plan.

But while reading the account of King Asa in 2 Chronicles this morning, I [Liz] was gently reminded that, because King Asa did what was good and right in the eyes of God, he prospered. It wasn't anything he did in his own strength – he just kept his eyes on the Lord. And unfortunately, at the end of his life, when he stopped trusting in God, he was afflicted with a disease and died. *(I'd love for you to read about King Asa and his reign in 2 Chronicles 14-16, and then come back and we will look at his life together.)*

In the beginning of King Asa's reign, he had his eyes set on God and did what was good and right. He got rid of the foreign altars so the people of Judah could no longer worship false gods, and he commanded Judah to seek the Lord and obey His commands. Once he did this, his kingdom was at peace. ***"No one was at war with him during those years, for the Lord gave him rest." 2 Chronicles 14:6***

When the Cushite army did try and attack King Asa, he called out to the Lord and said,

"Lord, there is no one like you to help the powerless against the mighty. Help us, O Lord our God, for we rely on You, and in your name we have come against this vast army. O Lord, You are our God; do not let man prevail against You." 2 Chronicles 14:11.

And what did the Lord do? He struck down the Cushites and gave King Asa and the people of Judah rest on every side.

Lately, when reading Scripture, I've been really trying to keep it simple, take it word for word, and make it applicable to my life. So if we break those verses down, King Asa was able to be at peace and have rest all around him not by worshipping false gods, but by calling out to the Lord and asking for help. I know we all want peace and rest all around us! So let's follow King Asa's example and keep God on the thrones of our hearts and not strive for things of this world. And let's call out to Him in our times of need. So often we turn to a self-help book or call a friend when what we really need to do is just cry out to Jesus!

In fact, it says in **2 Chronicles 15:12 and 15**: *"They entered into a covenant to seek the Lord, the God of their fathers, with all their heart and soul. All Judah rejoiced about the oath because they had sworn it wholeheartedly. They sought God eagerly, and he was found by them. So the Lord gave them rest on every side."*

Again, keeping this super-simple and applicable, I want to encourage you to take some time today and write a covenant with your Father, and make an oath that you will seek Him eagerly with your whole heart. I'm personally writing it in my journal and on my bathroom mirror so I can see it and be reminded of it. Because sisters, I want peace on every side of me! Don't you?

Sadly, at the end of King Asa's life, when he was confronted with an invasion from the northern kingdom, he stopped trusting wholeheartedly in the Lord. He actually hired the king of Aram to provide reinforcements rather than simply trust in the Lord. Then the prophet Hanani came to rebuke King Asa and reminded him that, *"The eyes of the Lord range throughout the earth to strengthen those whose hearts are fully committed to him. You have done a foolish thing, and from now on you will be at war."* 2 Chronicles 16:9

Instead of receiving that rebuke and using it to repent, King Asa was angry and put Hanani in prison. He was then afflicted with a disease in his feet and died. Sisters, that's not the way we want our story to end!

So today, instead of striving, worrying, comparing, or competing, let's keep our eyes on our Savior, call out to Him in our time of need, and wholeheartedly make an oath to seek Him with all of our hearts and souls! Then, get ready to have peace and rest on every side.

Dear God, I'm so grateful that I can cry out to You in my time of need. I seek You wholeheartedly with all of my heart and soul. I trust You to give me rest on every side. Instead of more striving, I just cry out to You today. Fill me with Your presence and Your peace. I love You. Amen.

94

SMALL

· ·

"We must never become so busy pursuing the growth of our business that we never pursue making ourselves less."

Michelle Myers

I [Michelle] have joked many times that the Apostle Paul is my Bible boyfriend. He's arguably the greatest missionary of all time, and his letters make up the majority of the New Testament. Not to mention, he somehow manages to use sarcasm without getting snarky.

When I think about Paul, many words and images come to mind.

I picture a bold man, bringing the gospel to the Gentiles. I'm filled with awe, imagining him worshiping in prison. I'm amazed as I consider his perseverance in his missionary journeys, not deterred by snake bites or shipwrecks.

But do you know what the name "Paul" means?

We'll get there, but first, a little backstory: Dual names were common during these days. Saul would have been his Hebrew name. Paul would have been his Roman name.

When I was growing up, I'm pretty sure I just assumed Jesus was the one who changed his name from Saul to Paul on the road to Damascus *(Acts 9:1-9)*. But after his conversion, he's still called Saul. Acts 13:9 is the first time we see Scripture record, ***"Saul, who was also called Paul..."***

From that verse on, he's always referred to as Paul.

Paul never discloses in any of his letters the reason for the name change. There's the practical argument that, as he went to proclaim the gospel to the Gentiles (everyone who wasn't Jewish), it would make sense for him to stop using his Hebrew name, Saul.

207

But there's also significance when we look at the meanings of these names.

Saul had a regal connotation. Historically, Saul was the name of the first king of Israel. But Paul meant something completely different.

Paul means *small* or *humble*.

Let that sink in for a second. The greatest missionary of all time who wrote the majority of the New Testament books *chose* to lay down his regal name and begin using the one that reminded him who he really was compared with his Savior:

Small.

Now, we can't draw any conclusions for certain *(I can't wait to ask him in Heaven one day!)* but doesn't it make sense to you that a man who used to spend his days persecuting Christians, who was once filled with pride and selfish ambition, would want the reminder every time his name was uttered that he must become less so that Christ can become greater *(John 3:30)*?

What a beautiful picture for us, friends.

Let's chat about the working world we live in. Everything is about becoming bigger: bigger platforms, bigger paychecks, bigger positions, bigger followings, etc., etc., etc.

But can I ask you to evaluate this:

How are you chasing small? What efforts are you making to become less so Christ can become greater?

Now, we don't all need to change our names to Paula. ;) But we do have to do *something*.

There's nothing wrong with being a good steward of your business and seeing growth. But there *is* a problem if we're so busy pursuing the growth of our business that we never pursue making ourselves less.

My pastor, Bruce Frank, made a phenomenal observation a few Sundays ago. He said, "The Bible doesn't tell us to pray for humility. But over and over again, it says 'Humble yourselves.'" *(A few reference points: Daniel 10:12, James 4:10, 1 Peter 5:6.)*

Just as we take action to grow our businesses, we must take action to pursue humility, as Paul *likely* did when he chose to change the primary name he used for himself.

How will you chase being smaller today so Christ can become greater? How will you pursue humility?

Chasing small just may create our greatest Kingdom impact. It certainly did for Paul.

God, there's a place for big and a place for small. But God, when it comes to how I am supposed to look in comparison to you, "bigger" has no place. My heart's cry, Lord, is to become less so You may become greater. Move me out of the way however You desire so my life points others to You. I love You. Amen.

95

DIVIDED FOCUS

. . . .

*"Our performance will never determine our outcome,
but our faithfulness WILL."*

Somer Phoebus

I [Somer] have personally been struggling in this season of life with the inability to focus in on one good thing.

You hear the business experts tell you that if you want to be successful, you have to go all in to the thing you're growing and that there's no "winning" if your attention is divided. I have a business mentor who has told me that multiple times.

Here's the thing: It makes sense and, for the most part, I believe it to be solid advice.

However, that is not what God is allowing in my life right now. At this time, my work life is made up of bouncing between three different areas of focus, three different teams, and three different sets of responsibilities, each that I am incredibly passionate about, and each that I know God has called me to.

Unfortunately, the question that the enemy has used to haunt/guilt me lately has been: "How much better could these ministries/businesses be if they had ALL of your attention?" It's a total punch in the gut, because that's impossible for me right now.

Until last night, I hadn't recognized it to be a question from the enemy or realized how deceptive it is. But in a series of God-ordained conversations, the Lord reminded me that He would never ask me that question, because my attention to a task list has absolutely nothing to do with my success. Don't get me wrong – it is imperative that we give our best to where He has us, but that's only because it's our responsibility as followers of Jesus to steward everything He gives us well. Our performance will never determine our outcome, but our faithfulness WILL.

"And let us not grow weary of doing good, for in due season we will reap, if we do not give up." Galatians 6:9

If you're struggling today with your assignment, whether you feel pulled in too many directions or exhausted because it's not the "ideal situation" that it seems everyone else has, don't jump ship too quickly. Instead of feeling discontent in a complicated circumstance, seek His face!

Get excited about chasing Jesus and let Him deal with the details.

Be faithful to His mission and let Him determine your next step.

Do everything you can do and do it to the best of your ability, but rest in the truth that His path to success looks entirely different than most.

Take the pressure to perform off your shoulders and just live like Jesus.

Our attention should be only on Jesus. Our hands can and should be busy in our work, but our eyes should never leave His face. Because as soon as they do, we can easily begin to forget that it isn't about the work, it's about Him.

God, I'm sorry for thinking that I know better than You do. Forgive me for trying to get ahead of Your plans for my life. God, help me to be diligent in my assignments from You and, in all that I do, I pray that You are glorified above everything else. Thank You for the lessons You teach us when we are waiting to hear from You. I love You! Amen.

96

PARTNER

. . . .

"It's not a choice whether or not to partner with God,
it's our responsibility."

Emily Copeland

First things first; as a Christ-follower, God is your boss no matter what your job is.

Colossians 3:23-24 says, ***"Whatever you do, work at it with all your heart, as working for the Lord, not for human masters, since you know that you will receive an inheritance from the Lord as a reward. It is the Lord Christ you are serving."***

If we all stood firm in working for God's glory, then our work spaces, organizations, and companies would know a whole lot more about Jesus than they do. I'll [Emily] be the first to admit that money has come before prayer and success before people more than I'd be comfortable to admit, but even then, I knew that I was solely responsible for making Him known in my world because He is my Father.

We can quickly see that we've made the wrong choice if we can say "yes" to any of these scenarios:

- We consult our professional development or podcast before God
- We'd rather get a few extra minutes of work in instead of getting into God's Word
- We care more about a customer's purchase than their knowledge of Jesus
- The greatest accomplishment that people see is our work, not in God's redemption of our lives
- Our greatest enthusiasm is in how our work has changed our life, not what God has done

The real choice that we are making when we choose not to partner with God is the choice of taking His glory and displaying it as if it is ours. We are telling Him that, even though He created us, set purpose on our lives, gave us gifts and talents, and also died to set our souls free, that following His lead isn't good enough.

Because of free-will (given by, you guessed it, God!), we do have a choice in front of us whether or not to ask God what He wants from us and then to follow His lead. But, in one final breath on the cross and with the words, "It is FINISHED", we live in the responsibility to give it all back to Him. It's just like being a parent. We have the choice to love our kids and raise them right, but it's always our responsibility whether or not we say yes to it.

We have to stop giving ourselves the choice to do the one thing that we were created for: to make God known.

Saying "yes" to the responsibility of partnering with God means:

Love Him Most

"And he said to him, 'You shall love the Lord your God with all your heart and with all your soul and with all your mind.'" **Matthew 22:37**

Pursue Him First

"But seek first the kingdom of God and his righteousness, and all these things will be added to you." **Matthew 6:33**

Trust His Plan

"Those who know your name trust in you, for you, LORD, have never forsaken those who seek you." **Psalm 9:10**

God, forgive us for making a choice out of the one thing You have created us for: to make You known. Your Name is worthy, and Your plan is greater. Give us courage not to look to the left or to the right, but to look to You for the next step. Take our work and use it for Your glory, not our own. We love You. Amen.

97

GOD'S PLAN

· ·

"We must begin to be women who believe more about
what God says than what we see, feel, or fear."

Jessica Hottle

After much deliberation about those who were still trying to obey the Law of Moses, Peter stands up to his feet and says: **"God who knows the hearts of every person, confirmed this when He gave them the Holy Spirit, just like He has given the Spirit to us. So now, not one thing separates us as Jews and Gentiles, for when they believe He makes their hearts pure. So why on earth would you now limit God's grace by replacing a yoke of duties on the shoulders of the believers that neither we nor our ancestors have been able to bear?" Acts 15:6-10**

If that last question wasn't enough, Peter asked one more, **"Don't you believe we are introduced to eternal life through the grace of our Lord Jesus – the same grace that has brought these people new life?"** (v. 11)

The response of the other apostles and elders? Silence.

My [Jessica] response? You can't stop God's plan!

We make the gospel complicated.

We make His love unreachable and unattainable based on our own sets of rules and experiences.

Even when it seems like a failure, it isn't.

Even when people unfollow you for sharing the message you are called to share, it's not because you are doing it wrong.

Even when it seems like the investments you have made don't seem to be coming back profitably, it's not that He doesn't see your time or effort.

We must begin to be women who believe more about what God says than what we see, feel, or fear.

The message above is the same for us. We no longer belong under duty and performance but under love and grace. Not one thing separates us from His love.

Like Dave Hesler recently said in his podcast about brave worship: "What if we spent more time worshipping than trying so hard?"

Let me encourage your heart today, friend, that even in the trials of business, life, being a mom, a wife, and so on, there's nothing we can do that can stop God's plan for our lives except to stop worshipping Him. It is as simple as that. But, not as easy as that.

So, let's be women who don't become like what we see, feel, or fear. Let's be women who release others into freedom – because your life is the key that unlocks it for them.

Sister, worship Him today more than anything else in your life.

Father, I pray for the release of any yoke of duty off my sister's life. Encourage her heart and remind her of the freedom she has in You. Remind her that we don't have to try so hard. Remind her that there's nothing she can do that will stop Your plan for her life. I love You. In Jesus name, Amen!

98

BROKENNESS

. . . .

"The sacrifices of God are a **broken** spirit;
a **broken** and contrite heart, O God, you will not despise."
Psalm 51:17

Liz Patton

When our oldest son moved up to the varsity baseball team this past spring, his coach met with all of the parents before the season got started. He very matter-of-factly stated, "When your son gets up to bat and strikes out, please do not say 'That's okay.' Because it's not okay." In that moment I [Liz] thought the coach sounded kind of harsh, but the more I thought about it, the more I realized that this statement is true not just in response to baseball, but also in response to my shortcomings and sins as well.

There is a very fine line between grace and brokenness when it comes to our sin. When we "strike out" in life, I think as Christians it's so easy to tell ourselves that God forgives us, He still loves us, and, because His grace covers a multitude of sins, it's all okay.

And yes, all those things are true. But I think we miss the point if we tell ourselves it's okay and just move along on our merry way. Because our sin is not okay. It should break us, and it should stir up a desire in us to pursue holiness – not more sin.

King David gives us the perfect example of this in Psalm 51 after he was confronted by the prophet Nathan for committing adultery with Bathsheba. David said to God:

"For you will not delight in sacrifice, or I would give it;
    you will not be pleased with a burnt offering.
*The sacrifices of God are a **broken** spirit;*
    *a **broken** and contrite heart, O God, you will not despise."*
(vs. 16-17)

216

As worldly people, we despise things that are broken. But not our loving God. His Word reassures us that a broken spirit and heart, He will NOT despise. Broken is how He wants us to come to Him.

When we come to God broken, not only does our brokenness draw us closer to Him, but it also allows us to be used by Him. Once we are broken before God, He is able to shape us and mold us into what He wants us to be. We are the clay, and He is our Potter.

Twice in God's Word, He refers to King David as being "a man after my own heart." God continued to love and to use David after his time of backsliding because David was broken AND repentant. Hear David's prayer:

"Have mercy on me, O God, according to your steadfast love; according to your abundant mercy blot out my transgressions. Wash me thoroughly from my iniquity, and cleanse me from my sin!" **Psalm 51:1-2**

Please hear my heart, sweet sister – God doesn't want us to walk around in shame and regret when we sin and fall short. But He also doesn't want us to cheerily gloss over our sin because we assume we've been covered by His grace. He wants us to come to Him broken and repentant. And when we do, He will put our broken pieces back together and love us into wholeness and relationship with Him once again.

Dear God, I am sorry for (insert specific sin here). Have mercy on me, and wash me whiter than snow. I come to You broken and ask You to please forgive me. I'm so thankful for Your son, Jesus, who was willing to die on the cross to save me from my sin. Thank You, Jesus, for taking my place. Father, You are the Potter, and I am the clay. Please put me back together again so I can be used by You and become a woman after Your own heart. I love You. Amen.

99

AN ETERNITY AT STAKE

. . . .

"Trying to discern the gospel through the world's view of it is like trying to read a book in pitch black darkness - it won't work."

Somer Phoebus

If you truly fear God, can you be a casual Christian?

I [Somer] really don't think so. At least, that's what God is revealing to me in His Word.

I'm not sure if you've noticed a theme in our *she works His way* communication lately, but our team is BURDENED for the casual Christian, the woman trying to discern the gospel through the world's view of it. That's like trying to read a book in pitch black darkness. The world's view of the gospel isn't anything like the gospel. Although, it sounds pretty, and it's the easiest kind of easy to live out, so I understand the draw to it.

A few weeks back, there was a post shared on our *she works His way* social media feed that stated so much truth. The feedback was mostly good, but of course there were a few who did not agree. But you know what they didn't agree with? It wasn't so much the idea of the quote, but the fact that in the quote there was a sentence that said (in response to us not doing something we should be doing as believers) "...there's something wrong with you." They were SO offended that anyone would say, "There's something wrong with you."

My friends, God's Word and His called servants that share it with us are here to encourage and spur on, but they're also commanded to share truth! ...To let us know when we are in fact WRONG. Which – spoiler alert – is often.

How did we get to this place where we have turned Jesus into some wimpy character in an old history book who walks around never stepping on toes and never speaking hard truth? If that's your view of Him, please open your Bible more because that is NOT who Jesus was or is. Yes, He loved in a bigger capacity than we will ever understand, but **because** of that love, He couldn't stand not to tell the truth. He loved people enough to make things uncomfortable.

218

Read John 3, the story of Jesus and Nicodemus. What an incredible example of an uncomfortable conversation leading to the truth of the gospel! Nicodemus was struggling to understand and listen to how Jesus responded:

Nicodemus said to him, "How can these things be?" Jesus answered him, "Are you the teacher of Israel and yet you do not understand these things? Truly, truly, I say to you, we speak of what we know, and bear witness to what we have seen, but you do not receive our testimony. If I have told you earthly things and you do not believe, how can you believe if I tell you heavenly things? No one has ascended into heaven except he who descended from heaven, the Son of Man. And as Moses lifted up the serpent in the wilderness, so must the Son of Man be lifted up, that whoever believes in him may have eternal life.

When you truly love someone, how can you let them walk in darkness? How can you let them believe lies? How can you let them pick and choose which part of the gospel they want to apply to their lives? Don't walk away from the conversation because it's hard...walk directly to it!

There is an eternity at stake here, friends, and that is so much more important to me than what others will think of me when they hear me speak against what God has called sin and speak for what God has called holy. But how can I speak of these things and also love people with the love of Jesus? That's where it's all gotten SO wonky! I speak this truth BECAUSE of my God-given love for His people, not in spite of it.

So ladies...

Will you study God's Word before you study a dynamic speaker's book?

Will you ask God for a discerning heart before you ask people for their opinions?

Will you love God's people enough to speak the truth before you back down to avoid an uncomfortable situation?

It's time! Here's your reminder today that there is a battle going on, one that's already won through Christ! So your only job is to pick a side and bring as many along as you possibly can! Will you do it?

God, show us the parts of our spiritual lives where we're too casual. Help us to see Your gospel for what it is and help us to share it with excitement and boldness. Thank You for Your Word that we have to guide us through these times where it's easy to get confused by the world. Help us to study and discern what is truth. We love You! Amen.

100

WORK CONFIRMS WORD

. . . .

"Look for evidence of His Word being confirmed as you work."

Michelle Myers

You can be an entrepreneur, work a corporate job, serve in the medical field or as a teacher or in any other occupation, but if you love Jesus, I [Michelle] typically find one thing all of you have in common when I meet you:

You feel all alone at work.

Whether it's because your main work hours are between naps and school pick-ups, at your kitchen table, that you're typically one of the only females in the room, or because you get mocked when you're the only one who doesn't laugh at dirty jokes in the break room, I find most women who identify with *she works His way* battle feeling isolated as they work.

That's why I may or may not have *(but definitely did!)* thrown a mini party at 5 a.m. when I found these two verses tucked into Mark:

"So then, when the Lord Jesus had spoken to them, He was received up into heaven and sat down at the right hand of God. And they [the disciples] went out and preached everywhere, while the Lord worked with them, and confirmed the word by the signs that followed." Mark 16:19-20

This is at the end of Jesus' ministry. At this point, Jesus has already died on the cross, defeated the grave through His resurrection three days later, and reappeared to the disciples. Now, He's given them their final instructions, and He ascends into Heaven to take His royal position at the right hand of the Father.

These two takeaways from verse 20 are too good to gloss over quickly:

1. As the disciples continued spreading His message everywhere, Jesus worked with them.

Everywhere. Jesus was with them everywhere…as they did His work.

Just to be clear: You do not have to have a ministry title to do ministry at work. And wherever you are bearing His name and His witness, you are doing His work.

And you're not alone. He is with you.

2. Their work confirmed God's message.

Your work, done in Jesus' name, for the glory of God, confirms God's Word. In almost two decades of the work-world across various industries, I'll tell you, there is nothing more exciting than getting a front row seat to watch God's truth come to life before you.

For example…

- To see God do immeasurably more than all we ask or imagine, according to His power at work within us *(Ephesians 3:20)*.
- To hope in the Lord and have Him renew your strength *(Isaiah 40:31)*.
- To see His power perfected in your weakness *(2 Corinthians 12:9)*.
- To see how God uses another believer to sharpen you *(Proverbs 27:17)*.
- To experience joy during hard times, knowing the testing of your faith produces endurance *(James 1:2-3)*.
- To see perfect love cast out fear *(1 John 4:18)*.
- To walk by faith, not by sight *(2 Corinthians 5:7)*.
- To love your enemies, do good to those who hate you, bless those who curse you and pray for those who mistreat you *(Luke 6:27-28)*.
- To see Light shine in the darkness *(John 1:5)*.
- To watch the Truth set free *(John 8:32)*.

Right? As I sit here and meditate on these verses, faces and memories come to mind in moments where I literally felt like I was watching the Bible leap off the page and come to life right in front of me.

But here's the catch: This doesn't happen if we're not *really* doing the work. Merely the right title or right knowledge doesn't automatically transfer to Kingdom work.

The disciples were **preaching everywhere** they went. *(This doesn't mean you need to stand on a chair in your office with a Bible in hand!)*

But if we pursue living out His message and sharing the truth that has transformed us with others, He joins us. When we pray to invite Him into our work because, in humility, we know that we are incapable of doing God's work without Him, He's there with us.

So in the moments when we feel alone, let's speak truth to our feelings and remind ourselves that Jesus is with us. And let's make sure that we are slowing down enough to recognize the moments when His work is happening right in front of us.

And finally, a good check for all of us: **Look for evidence of His Word being confirmed as you work.**

It will either serve as a.) your motivation to continue the work, or b.) your accountability that something about your words or actions needs to change to reflect Him more.

Let's get to work, *she works His way*. He's with us!

God, we can't thank You enough for the truth in Your Word to show us how to live. God, You don't have to use us, but You choose to. We are grateful to be able to serve as Your representatives in a world that desperately needs You. Help me to stay accountable to seeing Your Word confirmed as I work. Remind me often that Jesus is with me as I do Your work. I love You. Amen.

BUSINESS TRAINING
YOU CAN TRUST.

Join hundreds of women who are committed to
Christ, Their family, and their work...in that order.

For more information, visit
sheworksHISway.com